28/9/21

3

GW00854602

Ready to Lead

Text copyright © Ruth Hassall 2009
The author asserts the moral right
to be identified as the author of this work

Published by
The Bible Reading Fellowship
15 The Chambers, Vineyard
Abingdon OX14 3FE
United Kingdom
Tel: +44 (0)1865 319700
Email: enquiries@brf.org.uk
Website: www.brf.org.uk

ISBN 978 1 84101 620 7
First published 2009
10 9 8 7 6 5 4 3 2 1 0
All rights reserved

Acknowledgments
Unless otherwise stated, scripture quotations are taken from the Holy Bible, New Living
Translation, copyright © 1996, 2004. Used by permission of Tyndale House Publishers, Inc.,
Wheaton, Illinois 60189. All rights reserved.

Scripture quotations taken from the Contemporary English Version of the Bible, published by
HarperCollins Publishers, are copyright © 1991, 1992, 1995 American Bible Society.

Scripture quotations from THE MESSAGE. Copyright © by Eugene H. Peterson 1993, 1994, 1995.
Used by permission of NavPress Publishing Group.

A catalogue record for this book is available from the British Library

Printed in Singapore by Craft Print International Ltd

Ready to Lead

Growing Leaders – Youth Edition

Ruth Hassall

*To the young leaders of St Tee's,
my joy and my crown!*

(Philippians 4:1)

Contents

Introduction

In my diary I have a letter that I have carried around with me every day for the last 13 years. It's now looking dog-eared and worn and the words are pretty faded from having been read and re-read, and, to be honest, it's looking pretty grotty. However, that letter is one of the most important things that I own, partly because of who it's from and partly because of what's written in it.

You need to understand that leadership was never something that I had anticipated getting involved in. As a young teenager, I was far more willing to be led than ever to take the lead, in anything. Where others went, I followed. Yet something bizarre started to happen: other people seemed to see in front of them somebody who was completely different from the person I thought I was. Little by little, with their encouragement and their ability to see what I might become, my leadership journey began.

As I look back over the years that have passed since then (and there have been a few, though not that many!), it's amazing to see the way in which leadership opportunities have opened up—things that I could never, in my wildest dreams, have imagined. In fact, one of my mum's favourite phrases, when we look at different things that I've been part of, is, 'Well, who would have thought!' Not because they were opportunities that made headlines, but simply because I know that without God's intervention I would never have been part of them.

For me, youth and children's ministry has always been what's fired me. From a young age I was involved in youth and children's groups and it was within this area that I realized God was asking me to take a lead. So I started looking into how I could prepare for the role, and the answer seemed to be teacher training. It was really bizarre, as I knew I didn't want to be a teacher, but that was the option that seemed to fit best. So off I went to teacher training college, full of enthusiasm and excited about what the following years would hold.

The enthusiasm lasted for all of about six months, when I suddenly lost sight of why I was there, felt as if I was drowning in lesson plans, and couldn't think, for the life of me, what had prompted me to do this. I was ready to give it all up and make my way back home... when the letter arrived.

A friend, knowing something of what I was feeling, had written me the most timely letter that I have ever received. In it she reminded me of who I was as a child of God, she reflected on the skills and abilities that she could see in me, and she inspired me to look forward to what God had in store for me, taking me back to the Bible as the source of God's word and his promises. For me, that letter made all the difference. Today, I still read it because it is so full of wisdom and constantly points me back to God.

Throughout this book we're going to be looking at excerpts from another couple of letters. These letters were written in the same sort of vein as the one that I received. They are letters from an older Christian leader to a younger one, passing on all the wisdom and insight that he had gained over the years, and constantly pointing to God as the one who works through us in all that we do.

These letters were written by a man called Paul to a young friend of his, Timothy, and are found in the Bible, cunningly entitled 1 and 2 Timothy. We're going to take some time to unpack the wisdom and encouragement that Paul offers to Timothy and look at what we can learn from them for our leadership journey. What Paul had learnt in different situations he now wanted to pass on to Timothy, showing him what it means to be a godly leader.

The letters were written towards the end of Paul's life, so there's a sense of urgency about them. He wants to make sure that Timothy, although still quite young, knows that he is called by God to be a leader, and he wants to be sure that Timothy is well resourced in different aspects of leadership.

There are many possible reasons why you're reading this book. Maybe someone has given it to you as a present, having recognized in you an ability to lead others. Maybe you've picked it up yourself because you're already in a leadership role, you know that God has called you to be a leader and you want to grow as a leader. Maybe you don't see yourself as a leader at all, but there's something inside you that wants to find out more. Maybe you're in a leadership role in your school or sports team and are wondering what difference it should make that you're a Christian in that role.

Well, this book is written for you if you find yourself in any of those categories. Leadership is such an important issue, and one of the greatest privileges of my life has been to be part of the development of younger leaders. I worked for a number of years as a youth pastor and I know that some of the leaders who most inspired me were those members of the youth group who were responding to opportunities to lead. Their energy and vision for what God could do as we worked together was just incredible. A lot of what is written here comes from the journey that we took together as we looked at what it meant to be a young Christian leader in our homes, schools, colleges and churches.

I'm so glad that you're joining us too.

What is Christian leadership?

Dear Ruth

Hi! How are you? Was good to see you last week. I was wondering if you could help me with something? As you know, I've been helping out with the children's after-school club at the local primary school for almost a year now, which I really love. The thing is, the leaders have asked me if I'd like to be part of the team who run it. It's great to have been asked, but I'm not sure how to respond. I enjoy going along each week, and I've started organizing some of the games and leading some of the activities but I'm not sure that I could be one of the leaders. I mean, they're all so much older than me and I'm not sure that I'm a leader like them. What do you think I should do?

Look forward to hearing from you…

Mmmmmm, how to respond?

What do you think? Would you suggest…

○ that they shouldn't give it a second thought and say 'yes'?
○ that they wait until they're a bit older, because as a young person they can't really lead?
○ that they're right—because they're not like the other leaders, they shouldn't really join the team?

○ that they ask the leaders why they've been invited to be a leader?
○ that they talk to their parents or another adult about it?
○ something else?

There is no shortage of ideas on who or what is a leader. Many people are willing to be very vocal on their thoughts about what makes a good or, more often, a bad leader. The press is full of stories about those who we feel are failing in their roles as leaders, whether they're football managers, politicians, bank managers or church leaders.

Many would agree (both those within the church and those in the business world) that one of the greatest leaders of all time was Jesus. Here was one man who gathered together the most unlikely group of people and turned the world of his day upside down through his teaching and actions—and he continues to do so today. With some two billion people still following him today right across the world, it's hard to argue that Jesus isn't a great leader.

Spiritual giants?

As you begin this book, you may have questions in your mind about whether you really are a leader and whether God can use you to make a difference among your friends, in your school, at your church, on your sports team or whatever situation you may find yourself in. We can tend to think that God uses people we think of as spiritual giants—those who get up before it's light and pray for hours before the rest of us even make it out of bed, those who are strong and confident and never have a moment's doubt about their ability to lead. You may feel that you fit into that 'giants' category, and if you do, excellent—you may be highly confident about your leadership ability and wonder what this book could possibly have to offer you. Can I suggest that you suspend judgment for a moment and keep reading? However, my guess is that most of us don't feel that way, yet would love for God to use us to lead people for him and to him.

The great news is that throughout history God has chosen people like you and me to be those that he uses in leadership roles. Let's take a quick wander through the Bible and have a look at some of the leaders we meet along the way:

Moses

If there was anyone who really didn't consider himself to be a leader, it was Moses. In Exodus 3 and 4 we overhear an ongoing conversation between Moses and God, as God calls Moses to lead the people of Israel out of slavery in Egypt and Moses gives many excuses as to why he's not the man for the job. His first excuse is that he's not the right person to stand before Pharaoh. Next, he doesn't think the people will believe him when he says that God has sent him, and finally he launches in with the argument that he's not a good speaker—very clumsy with words, so obviously not the right choice. At this point God gets a bit annoyed with Moses and agrees to let his brother Aaron act as his spokesperson. But God is adamant that it is Moses who is to lead the people, despite all his arguments. And he does!

Deborah

Deborah played a unique role in the life of the people of Israel. She was the first and only female military leader in the Old Testament, and her story is found in Judges 4 and 5. The people of Israel were suffering badly under the rule of King Jabin, who had invaded their land. He was a violent and harsh ruler and the people were desperately afraid and unhappy. Unable to take this any more, Deborah calls the people to action and, under her command, another military leader, Barak, gathers together an army of 10,000 men.

Deborah calls the army to the top of Mount Tabor and King Jabin quickly follows. The Israelite troops charge down the mountain and drive

King Jabin and his army into the River Kishon, where they get stuck and are rendered completely powerless. Excellent! This is what the people of Israel said about Deborah: 'There were few people left in the villages of Israel—until Deborah arose as a mother for Israel' (Judges 5:7).

Esther

Did you know that Esther is the only book in the Bible that never mentions God? Yet God is at work in the most amazing ways throughout the story of Esther's life and the lives of the Jewish people. God chooses this young Jewish woman to outwit the Persian king's evil right-hand man, Haman, who is intent on wiping out the Jewish people. Risking her own life, she steps up to the challenge and takes on the enemy of her people—and wins!

David

God's people, the nation of Israel, decided that what they really needed in order to live well was a king. Until this point they had had a number of judges (people like Deborah and Samson, whom you might also have come across in the Old Testament), but they felt that this system wasn't working and a king would do a much better job.

So the last judge, Samuel (whom God spoke to in the temple when he was a young boy), goes to find them a king. First, he anoints a man called Saul as king, but that doesn't turn out very well, so God tells him to go to a man called Jesse, who has eight sons. One of these young men is to be the chosen king.

In 1 Samuel 16 we read how Samuel goes to Jesse and asks to meet his sons. One after another they are presented before Samuel, but none of them is the one that God wants. Samuel can't quite understand what's going on because, to his mind, they're all good men, strong and courageous, but God reminds Samuel that his way of choosing is different from others'. While people look at the outward appearance, God is far more concerned about what is happening on the inside, how their heart is (v. 7). Finally the youngest son is brought out, a young shepherd boy that his father has almost forgotten about, and God says to Samuel, 'Yes, this is the one that I want you to anoint as king.'

Gideon

The story of Gideon has to be one of my favourites. Gideon is threshing wheat in a winepress, trying to stay hidden from the hostile raiders who are harassing Israel at the time. Without any kind of warning, the angel of the Lord appears to him and greets him by saying, 'Mighty hero, the Lord is with you!' (Judges 6:12).

Gideon has to do a double take to see who the angel is talking to! Him, Gideon, a strong and mighty hero? His clan is the weakest of all the clans, and within his clan he is the weakest person. How can he be the one that God will use to rescue the people of Israel from their enemy, the Midianites? But he was God's choice and he did exactly what God had promised—ran the enemy right out of town. (See Judges 7 for the full story.)

It would seem that the Bible is full of people who didn't really recognize themselves as leaders, yet God chose them and used them anyway. And he continues to do so. Here's Sarah's story:

I never would have thought of myself as a leader, but as a teenager I was encouraged to get involved in leading on holiday clubs and, later, on youth camps. I would completely recommend taking up these opportunities as, being quite a shy person growing up, they gave me so much confidence in myself and highlighted abilities I didn't even know I had. I'm now in my 20s, still involved in youth leadership. I've grown so much in speaking to large groups, working with new people, and now have such an excitement in seeing potential arise in the next generation of leaders.

Definitions of leadership

Before we go any further, I think it's worth taking a few moments to think through what we mean when we talk about leadership. Often, the images we have in our minds of what a leader is will influence us in our understanding of what it means to be a leader. They might even stop us from taking up the leadership challenge because we don't think we match those images.

Think about these four questions for a moment.

○ What words come into your mind when you hear the word 'leader'?
○ Who do you think of when you're asked to think of a leader?
○ Who is the leader who has most influenced you? (It could be someone famous or someone from your local situation.)
○ What is it about this person, do you think, that makes them a good leader?

I asked a few of the teenagers in my church a couple of these questions. Here are some of their responses to question 1:

A leader is...
○ '... someone who shows people what to do'.
○ '... someone people listen to, respect and learn from'.
○ '... someone others follow'.
○ '... someone who takes charge and inspires people'.
○ '... someone who makes things run smoothly and properly in a certain situation'.
○ '... someone who inspires those around them to achieve their potential'.

As you can see, people have varying views on what a leader is. Throughout history, people have studied this subject. Here are a few definitions that others have given:

A leader is 'the person who leads or commands a group, organization or country'.
OXFORD ENGLISH DICTIONARY

My definition of a leader... is one who can persuade people to do what they don't want to do, or do what they're too lazy to do, and like it.
HARRY S. TRUMAN, US PRESIDENT 1945–53

Leadership occurs when one person induces others to work toward some predetermined objectives.
ROBERT K. MASSIE, PRESIDENT OF THE AUTHORS' GUILD 1987–91

Leadership is the ability of a superior to influence the behaviour of a subordinate or group and persuade them to follow a particular course of action.
CHESTER IRVING BARNARD (1886–1961), PRESIDENT OF NEW JERSEY BELL TELEPHONE COMPANY AND THE ROCKEFELLER FOUNDATION

Leadership is the art of influencing and directing people in such a way that will win their obedience, confidence, respect and loyal cooperation in achieving common objectives.
US AIR FORCE

If your actions inspire others to dream more, learn more, do more and become more, you are a leader.
JOHN QUINCY ADAMS, US PRESIDENT 1825–29

The truth of the matter is that there is no one type of person who is a leader. Leaders come in all sorts of shapes and sizes, so rather than thinking who or what is a leader, perhaps it would be more helpful to define what leadership is made up of.

Here are three key things that leadership is about: influence, role and ability.

Influence

At its most basic, leadership is about influence. On this level, pretty much all of us are leaders as we all have the opportunity to influence other people—whether for good or for bad. So the first question to ask is, 'Do I influence other people?' However, there is more to leadership than influence alone.

Role

A great way of growing in leadership is to have a role of responsibility. That might mean helping to lead a children's group in your church, being captain of your sports team, leading a peer cell group, taking on the role of class president or any number of other situations where you find yourself taking on a lead role.

We can read about leadership, and that's always useful and a great way to learn, but to learn to lead properly we need to have a go at leading.

Leadership, like swimming, cannot be learned by reading about it.
HENRY MINTZBERG

As a teenager, I was very shy and never imagined myself as a leader at all. Every year in the church where I grew up, we held a holiday club for children from the surrounding villages. This had run for a number of years and I'd helped out at it a good few times. Then one year we hit a bit of a problem: the guy who usually led the holiday club had moved to a different part of the country so was no longer able to continue in that role. A new leader needed to be found. I was completely stunned when the minister asked me and another teenager if we would take on the overall leadership for the event. To be honest, I was scared silly. I did a pretty good imitation of Moses in the excuses department, and my friend was close behind. However, in the end we both took on the role and, looking back, I am so grateful for that opportunity because it was a key time for me in growing as a leader.

A number of years later, I was working as youth pastor in a church and we had started running holiday clubs in our town. Again, all was going smoothly until the week before the event was to happen. Out of the blue, I was struck down with appendicitis. There was a fair amount of panic—who was going to lead it now? I got together (in my hospital bed) with a few other members of the team, and we agreed that the best person to take my place was Jonny, a 16-year-old church member. He had served faithfully as part of the team for years, he knew how it worked and what needed to be done, and we felt he had the skills needed to lead the team. He did a brilliant job—in fact, in my opinion, too good a job, as I had a hard time convincing the team that I should come back! Now in his 20s, Jonny looks back to that time as a key experience for his growth in leadership.

So we have influence and we have a role to play. It doesn't end there, though. I guess we can all think of people who have a leadership role but who aren't particularly good at it. I started training as a primary school teacher and on one of my teaching placements I was put in a class with a teacher (who shall remain nameless) who very obviously didn't like children. She had the role of leadership but I'm not convinced that she was the right person for it. That's because, along with the role, we need something else.

Ability

Ability is made up of a number of different things.

❍ **Skills:** things that you can learn to do through training—for example, learning how to put a good team together for a football match or how to lead a Bible study.

❍ **Knowledge:** things you can learn in theory. A key part of gaining knowledge is learning to ask good questions, and then listening to the answers.

❍ **Talents:** particular gifts that you have, like being musical or sporty or great at maths. A helpful way of understanding a talent is that it's not necessarily something you can do, it's what you can't help yourself doing.[1] For instance, if I'm in a small group that's meant to be doing something, and nobody takes a lead, I just can't help myself doing just that. Maybe, for you, it's making people feel welcome, or being unable to resist turning anything and everything into a football. The interesting thing about talents is that they are generally formed in us by the time we reach our late teens. During your childhood and teenage years, you can continue to develop new talents, but research has shown that once you are over 20 it becomes incredibly hard to develop a new talent. This is really bad news for those of us who passed the 20 mark some time ago, but for you it means there are still opportunities to develop in new areas. So this is a great time for you to be thinking about leadership and trying out new things.

The combination of these things—skills, knowledge and talents—makes up your ability.

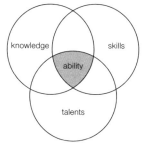

To grow as leaders, we need to be people of good influence, we need to have an appropriate leadership role and we need to be growing in our leadership ability by adding to our skills and knowledge and developing our talents. We'll be looking at how we do this in Chapter 5.

Distinctives of Christian leadership

To sum up so far, then, leaders come in all sorts of shapes and sizes, a range of personality types and with different gifts and skills. Leadership is about being able to influence others positively, having a role to play and growing in the ability to play that role.

We need to take this a step further, though. If we are serious about being a Christian leader, then we need to look closely at Jesus' leadership requirements for those who follow him.

Christian leadership is not just about leading in church groups or services. If you are a Christian and are growing in leadership, then you are a Christian leader wherever you find yourself. One of the aims of this book is to explore how we can be Christian leaders in all the different roles that we play. What does it mean to be a sports captain, or a head girl, who is a Christian? Does it differ from the way we lead in what we see as 'Christian' situations? In fact, wherever we lead, we will always be a Christian leader by virtue of the fact that we are following Christ. So what does a Christian leader look like?

When Jesus talks about leadership, there is only one word that he repeatedly uses. For Jesus, being a leader is about being a servant. He makes this very clear to his disciples in a number of situations.

One day the mother of two of Jesus' disciples, James and John, came to ask him if her boys could sit in the places of honour in his kingdom. This was Jesus' response: 'You know that in this world kings are tyrants, and officials lord it over the people beneath them. But among you it should be quite different. Whoever wants to be a leader among you must be your servant, and whoever wants to be first must become your slave' (Matthew 20:25–27, NLT, 1996).

'Among you it should be quite different.' Jesus was turning everything they'd ever known upside down. To be a leader in his kingdom, as one of his followers, they needed to be prepared to serve. This was radically different from the leadership they'd experienced from the people around them. Surely, leadership was about power and authority and ordering people around? But Jesus was saying something quite different.

It's interesting that when Jesus wanted to teach the disciples something, he often used stories or parables to make his point. When he was teaching them about leadership, though, he didn't tell a story. He acted it out for them:

Jesus knew that the Father had given him authority over everything and that he had come from God and would return to God. So he got up from the table, took off his robe, wrapped a towel around his waist, and poured water into a basin. Then he began to wash the disciples' feet, drying them with the towel he had around him. (John 13:3–5)

Can you imagine how the disciples must have felt? Here was Jesus, the Son of God, the one who had healed the sick, raised the dead and taught the crowds, kneeling in front of them and washing away the dirt of the day, taking on the role of the servant. Jesus made it very clear in Matthew 20:28 that this was why he had come: his purpose was to serve, and ultimately this would lead him to the cross, where he would serve the greatest need of all people—providing a way for them to be right with God.

In Jesus' mind, serving and leading were totally connected. He wanted his followers to be very clear that this was what leadership should be about for them, too:

After washing their feet, he put on his robe again and sat down and asked, 'Do you understand what I was doing? You call me "Teacher" and "Lord", and you are right because that's what I am. And since I, your Lord and Teacher, have washed your feet, you ought to wash each other's feet. I have given you an example to follow. Do as I have done to you.' (John 13:12–15)

Serving others is at the heart of Christian leadership, not just for the first disciples but for us today. The apostle Paul emphasized this when he challenged the Christians at Philippi about their behaviour: 'You must have the same attitude that Christ Jesus had. Though he was God, he did not think of equality with God as something to cling to. Instead, he gave up his divine privileges; he took the humble position of a slave and was born as a human being' (Philippians 2:5–7).

If we want to be leaders, we really need to understand this: we need to learn to lead like Jesus, by serving others. As we do this, not only will we have the chance to lead but we'll also have the chance to change the nature of leadership in our churches, our schools, our homes and our teams. Leadership, in Jesus' opinion, is not an opportunity to exert power and boss others around: it's an opportunity to serve.

But let's just press the pause button for a moment. Being a servant leader does not mean that we take any and every opportunity to literally wash people's feet! That was just the example that Jesus gave because it was appropriate in his context. The 12.5es knew that he was 'Teacher' and 'Lord'. They also knew that washing feet was the task reserved for the lowest of all servants. Jesus was trying to demonstrate to them that the two go together. Secondly, being a servant leader does not mean that we do whatever anybody asks of us. There were times when Jesus said 'no' to people because, as servant leaders, we're serving God first and foremost, so we do what he asks of us. What could this sort of leadership look like for us? Here are a few examples:

◯ The captain of the cricket team, having led his team in victory, returns to the club house with players and parents and is the first to take round the sandwiches, ensuring that everyone has something to eat.
◯ The person leading the children's group stays behind to wash up the glue sticks and paintbrushes that have been left in a sticky state.
◯ The avid footballer, desperate to get outside for a kickabout, chooses to stay in to help a little brother with his homework.
◯ The head girl, rather than getting younger pupils to clear litter in the playground, goes around and clears it up herself.

Do you get the idea? Yes, leadership is about upfront stuff, it's about leading the way, but it's also about being willing to play the role of the one who serves others.

Definition of Christian leadership

As we come to the end of this first chapter, before moving on to a deeper understanding of leadership, I thought it might be helpful to pull it all together into a definition of what we mean by Christian leadership. It is:

... an attitude of servanthood
   ... using the ability that God has given
      ... to lead others in a way that shows God's love
         ... and achieves God's goals.

Christian leadership isn't about position or power; it's about serving God and others. The challenge is to keep growing and learning and looking for ways in which you can lead through serving others.

Wrapping it up

So, are you a leader? I hope that, after reading this chapter, you will have seen that there is no one type of person that is a leader. Above all, God is looking for those who are willing to serve others; in his mind, those are the real leaders. Is that you? Would you like it to be? If so, read on—God has great adventures in store for you!

Ready to lead

To think about:

○ Has your understanding of leadership changed in any way? If so, how?
○ As you think through your week, what opportunities do you have to serve others?

To do:

○ Write out the definition of Christian leadership (or your own interpretation of it) and put it somewhere so that you'll notice it often.
○ Find a friend or another leader whom you can talk to about what you're reading in this book.

2

First a follower

Hi Ruth

Yeah, sorry to have missed you too this last couple of Sundays. I had planned to come to church this week but I'm afraid life just took over! On Tuesday I was leading my peer cell group, on Wednesday it was worship group practice and on Friday I was leading an evangelistic event at school, so by the time I got to Sunday I really needed to catch up on my homework.

Really loving the things that I'm doing but have to admit it is pretty exhausting. I guess it's great, though, that I have so many opportunities to serve God—racking up my points in heaven!

Thanks for the Bible reading notes you sent with my mum. You might want to give them to someone else because I haven't started last month's yet.

Cheers…

Mmmmmm, how to respond?

What do you think? Would you suggest...

○ that they rejoice about being so mightily used by God?
○ that they take a bit of time out to reflect on their own relationship with God?

- ○ that they hide their Bible reading notes somewhere, so as not to feel guilty every time they spot them?
- ○ that they talk to their youth leader about cutting back on some of the activities?
- ○ that they think about what the Bible says about taking Sunday as a day off?
- ○ something else?

'But you, Timothy, are a man of God...'

1 TIMOTHY 6:11

Have you ever had one of those days when you wish you could start all over again? I think I've had more than I care to remember, but one that sticks in my mind is the day when a colleague, Penny, and I were travelling over to Ireland to do a training event for some youth and children's leaders.

The plan had been that I would collect Penny, we'd make our way to the airport in plenty of time to check our bags in and then we'd go and have a leisurely breakfast before boarding the plane, where we would just relax and enjoy the flight, arriving rested and refreshed in Belfast ready to do a day's training. That was the plan.

Sadly, the reality was very different. It all started to go wrong at the starting point. I overslept! To this day, I'm not quite sure how that happened. Rarely do I oversleep, and especially not on the night before a training event. But on this day I did—somehow, still in my sleep, I turned my alarm off. Not the best of starts.

So I dashed madly around, thinking that at least I'd have time to sort myself out at the airport. I arrived late at Penny's (of course, she'd been ready for quite a while, so was not best pleased) and we headed for the airport. But that day there were major roadworks to get snarled up in. We got to the airport car park as the shuttle bus was just pulling out. Having waited for the next bus, we arrived at the check-in with barely minutes to spare.

We ran through to the desk like a pair of mad women, not realizing that we'd chosen the desk with the trainee on it. In horror I watched as he pressed the button to send my luggage off while still holding the destination label in his hand. Yet more running as we chased my suitcase along the conveyor belt's path to rescue it before it got lost in the huge melee that is the luggage sorting depot. Finally we made it on to the plane, hot and dishevelled, and arrived in Belfast in a far from serene state.

So what has this got to do with leadership? Well, the issue is that if we want to be godly leaders, then our starting point really matters. Get that wrong and the knock-on effect is pretty dramatic. If we want to be leaders in God's kingdom, we need to get our starting point absolutely right. That's why, before we get into the more practical details of being a leader, we're going to take a couple of chapters to lay some more foundations that will provide a good building ground.

As I mentioned in the Introduction, throughout this book we'll be looking at some of the advice that Paul gave his friend Timothy about growing as a leader. In 1 Timothy 6:11, having warned Timothy about people who follow false teachers and those that are just concerned about money and wealth, Paul makes this statement: 'But you, Timothy, are a man of God; so run from all these evil things.' It's as if he's saying to Timothy, 'To avoid getting caught up in these things, you need to remember who and whose you are. You belong to God, so your life should be different.' If we forget that as our starting point, it's not long before we find ourselves in trouble.

If we're serious about growing in leadership, we need to take the time to remember who and whose we are. If we get that starting point wrong, we'll start doing everything in order to earn other people's approval—which is just exhausting, and gets in the way of listening to God. Above and beyond anything else, we are God's people, his children, and that needs to be our starting point.

I'm so glad that you're thinking about leadership. Our schools, communities and churches desperately need good leaders—but God's intention is that, as you lead other people, you make it your priority to follow him closely. It's amazing how quickly we can find our identity in the roles that we play rather than in God. If we want to be safe people to follow, then we need first to be followers, disciples of Jesus. That is what God cares about most of all.

This is something that we need to keep returning to, because we can all too quickly move away from our starting point. And often it's not bad things that distract us; very often, it's good things.

On this subject of distractions, one of my most sobering moments happened as I was driving a minibus full of young people home from a weekend away in the Lake District. We'd had a fantastic time together and it was so good to hear the chatting and singing and laughter coming from the group. We'd been travelling for a little while when one of the group leant forward to talk to me. She told me that she'd just been praying for me and felt that God wanted me to know that he loved the role I played as youth pastor, and he loved the concern that I had for the group, but he'd really like to meet Ruth again.

As I reflected, I realized that she was right. Whenever I opened my Bible, it was to prepare teaching for the group. Whenever I prayed, it was to pray for the members of the group. My whole identity had become that of 'youth pastor', and God had to remind me that, first and foremost, I was Ruth, disciple of Jesus. It's not that what I was doing was wrong, it's just that I'd got my starting point wrong.

When my identity is caught up in what I do and the role that I play, it's very easy for me to make wrong decisions, because I'm listening to the wrong voices. When my identity is centred in God, it's easier for me to hear his voice and do what he is asking of me.

You might want to stop for a moment and think about what your starting point is right now. What are the roles that you play? Where do you think your identity lies?

Life beyond youth group

An interesting thing happens when people get too old to be in their youth group, or if they leave to go to university or take a job somewhere else. Some of them stay committed to God and continue growing in their relationship with him, even though the rest of the group aren't around any more and they don't have their youth leader to encourage them. Others, however, seem to end their commitment to God when youth group ends. What is it that makes the difference?

A couple of months ago, I was talking about this with some people who had come out of youth group and had recently gone to university. As we talked, it appeared that the difference between those who had stayed committed to God and those who hadn't was about whether they had learnt to spend time with God on their own so that they were not dependent on their friends or youth group to buoy them up. Many of them had experienced spiritual growth while they had belonged to a youth programme and had people around who would ask them questions about their relationship with God. But they hadn't built their own spiritual foundations for their lives, so their faith seemed to crumble once the support was removed and the people were no longer there.

In John 15, Jesus makes some interesting statements about our relationship with God. I suggest you put this book down and have a look at verses 1–17. Over and over again, Jesus says that we need to 'remain' in him and realize that without him we can 'do nothing' (v. 5). Those are strong statements and, if you're anything like me, at the back of your mind you're wondering if that statement is really true. Can I really do nothing? I can think of plenty of things that I can do, but the point Jesus is making is that if you want to do anything of lasting value, anything that is fruitful for God's kingdom, then it can only happen if you remain close to God. Within the passage, Jesus mentions three essentials for a fruitful, godly life.

○ **It's about abiding:** if we want to keep Christ as our starting point, then we need to stay close and connected to him.

○ **It's about love:** we can genuinely love each other and God only when we understand his amazing love for us. Knowing that God has chosen us to be his people assures us of his love. This means that, rather than having to work constantly to make him love us, we can be people who work from his love, letting that love flow out to others. This may seem a very subtle distinction, but it makes a world of difference if we start by truly knowing God's love for us. It makes us less driven, less desperate to prove ourselves and more confident in our identity in Christ.

○ **It's about obedience:** we respond to God's love for us by being obedient to what he asks of us. He wants our obedience, not to make life difficult or dull but, as Jesus says, 'that my joy may be in you and your joy may be complete' (v. 11).

That's that, then. It's all very easy: we stay close to God and know his love, and out of that knowledge we serve him, his people and the world. If only it were that simple! Again, it's back to the starting point: how do we stay close to God? There are so many things that demand our attention, so many voices telling us what we should be and do, that God's voice gets drowned out.

This isn't a new challenge. Christians through the centuries have struggled with the question of how to stay close to God. I have a friend, John, who is now in his 90s and has been a Christian since he was a teenager. I asked him what it is that has helped him stay close to God for nearly 80 years, as his relationship with God is so vibrant and he inspires my own faith so much. His response was the same as that of thousands and thousands of faithful Christians throughout history: 'I exercise spiritual disciplines.'

Now, to be honest, that doesn't sound like a lot of fun, does it? Discipline isn't a word that makes any of us jump for joy! It may sound like just keeping a load of rules, but it's really more about training. Paul talks to Timothy about this, too. He says: 'Do not waste time arguing over godless ideas and old wives' tales. Instead, train yourself to be godly. "Physical training is good, but training for godliness is much better, promising benefits in this life and in the life to come"' (1 Timothy 4:7–8).

Here's a helpful way of thinking about it: imagine that you decide you want to run a marathon. If you set out to run a marathon tomorrow without any training, no matter how hard you tried, you almost certainly wouldn't be able to make it round the full 26 miles of the course. However, if you knew that you were going to run a marathon in six months' time, you could establish a training routine that might enable you to succeed.

We can try really hard to stay close to God, but we will have little success. We do well for a week or so, but it soon peters out. What we need to do is train ourselves to hear God, to know what he is asking us to do, and to be led by him. That's where the spiritual disciplines come in. It's like developing spiritual muscle.

I pressed my friend John a bit further and asked him what he meant by exercising spiritual disciplines. He told me that the four things that had been really important to him over the years were these:

○ Reading the Bible
○ Spending time in prayer
○ Meeting with God's people
○ Serving others

These are all spiritual disciplines, and they're vital for us, too, if we are going to stay close to God and be followers of Jesus.

Engaging with the Bible

The Bible is the most amazing book, and God has promised to speak to us through it. Authors Dorothy Bass and Don Richter say this:

I tremble and give thanks every time I read the Bible. God meets us on these pages and awakens us to a world more broken and more blessed than we imagined. If you love your life just as it is right now, forget about the Bible. Entering the biblical story, the story of God's self-giving love, and living among other people shaped by it, could be dangerous. When you get into this story, it will get into you and begin shaping how you live. When you think of yourself as part of this story, you will hear God speaking words of warning and comfort to you. Let yourself get lost in this story, and you will find yourself drawn into a new way to live.[2]

I love that line: 'When you get into this story, it will get into you and begin shaping how you live.' That is God's intention for us. He wants the Bible to shape the way that we live, not just to be information that might come in useful if we appear on *Who Wants to Be a Millionaire?* If we want to be able to make good decisions and live in a way that pleases God, we need to know what he has to say. The best way to know that is to get into the Bible.

There are many resources around to help us to do this—including Bible reading notes, study guides, and Bible reading websites. It's important to find something that is helpful to you, recognizing that we all learn in different ways. Why not ask some older Christians how they spend time in the Bible? You could also see if some friends would like to meet together to discuss what you've been reading.

In the youth group that I was part of, every year we were thrown the challenge of reading the whole Bible in twelve months. Being the competitive sort, I loved this kind of challenge and was determined to do it. So, day after day, I read diligently through my Bible, and by the end of the year I had read the whole lot. The only problem was that I couldn't really remember much of it. I'd been so busy simply trying to get through it that I hadn't let any of it sink in or change the way I thought about things.

Please don't get me wrong: reading the Bible in a year is a great thing to do, but I think God is far more concerned that by reading his word I have met with him and been changed than that I receive the trophy for making it all the way through to the end of Revelation.

Prayer

Prayer is one of the greatest privileges that human beings have, yet it is often one of the hardest things to do. We get distracted, fall asleep or simply don't get round to it. We end up feeling guilty, knowing that it's something we should do, but the guilt only leads to more inaction. Thomas Merton was a well-known 20th-century author and monk, who said this about prayer: 'The great thing is prayer. Prayer itself. If you want a life of prayer, the way to get it is by praying. You start where you are and you deepen what you already have.'[3]

His advice is so good! Start where you are. If you find it difficult to pray, deciding to pray for an hour each day is likely to lead to disappointment. It's better to start by committing to pray for maybe five or ten minutes and gradually letting the time increase day by day.

Find a place where you can be quiet, without distractions. It's often helpful to use the same place each day, as simply being there will send messages to your brain that praying is what you're there to do. Take a couple of minutes to be quiet and focus on God. You might like to listen to a song that helps you focus, or write your thoughts down. Sometimes, when I'm feeling distracted, I write my prayers down and wait for God to respond. Then I write down his response, too.

There are different types of prayer, and, as we grow in our relationship with God, it's good to grow in the way that we pray. Here are some of the different ways in which we can pray:

○ **Praise and worship:** simply telling God how great he is. I often start with a psalm to get me into the right frame of mind, and then I continue just telling God what I think is great about him. When we worship God, we take our eyes off ourselves and focus them on something bigger, giving us a different perspective.
○ **Asking:** bringing our requests to God—whatever we're concerned about and want God's help with.
○ **Intercession:** praying for others—our friends, families and situations around the world.

○ **Confession:** talking to God about the things that we didn't get right, asking for his forgiveness and his help to grow.

It's really important to remember that prayer is not about duty, though. It's about relationship—our relationship with God. God loves it when we meet with him and take time to talk with him about everything that is going on in our lives, and when we ask him what's on his heart. The following two quotations paint a good picture of why prayer is such an important part of our day.

The very moment you wake up each morning... all your wishes and hopes for the day rush at you like wild animals. And the first job of each morning consists simply in shoving them all back; in listening to that other voice, taking that other point of view, letting that other, larger stronger, quieter life come flowing in.[4]

Jesus taught that the most important part of prayer is being persistent (see Luke 18:1–8). The more we continue to pray, the more our heart opens for receiving and giving love. Try to continue the same prayer practice even when you get bored or tired of it. Praying is a little like playing an instrument or being an athlete: it takes practice. Over time you'll discover that your prayer time will begin to transform you. You may notice a greater sense of peace, a deeper longing to help others, a greater hunger to be with God, a stronger sense of who you are. These are natural fruits of spending time with God.[5]

Meeting with God's people

In a word, church! We were never created to follow Jesus by ourselves. We need each other. An illustration of this that has stuck with me since I heard it is the example of a piece of coal. When a piece of coal is on a lit fire, it gets incredibly hot and stays that way. However, if it falls out of the fire and on to the hearth, it goes cold in a matter of minutes. We need each other to encourage us in our relationship with God. We need people who remind us of God's promises when we're going through difficult times. We need people who will remind us who we are and who God is at the times when we can't feel his closeness. And we need to be that person for others.

Serving others

This takes us back to Chapter 1: as followers of Jesus, we need to do what Jesus did, which was to serve others. Our service doesn't always have to be in major ways, but we should always be on the lookout for ways in which we can serve those around us. Someone once told me that a huge part of being a leader is moving chairs, and he was right. Obviously that's not what it's all about, but this person was trying to challenge me about whether I'd be willing to serve in quiet, hidden ways—ways that many people wouldn't see and wouldn't thank me for. If I wasn't willing to do that, then I probably wasn't ready for leadership.

Wrapping it up

As we come to the close of this chapter, you might like to take some time to think over some of the issues we've looked at. The following questions might be useful to help you do that.

Your relationship with God
❍ How would you describe your relationship with God?
❍ When and how did you come to faith?
❍ Do you spend time on your own, reading your Bible and praying?
❍ What are these times like? How would you like to see them get better?
❍ In what ways do you feel that you have a friendship with God?

○ What are the doubts or questions that you struggle with?
○ What have been the highlights or milestones in your journey of faith?

Your relationship with others

○ How are your relationships with friends and family?
○ How are they affected by your relationship with Christ?
○ Who are your closest friends?
○ How do you respond to the needs you see around you?
○ How does your faith help you to be loving and forgiving?
○ Do you belong to a church? If so, what do you appreciate about it? If not, why not?

Your relationship with yourself

○ How do you respond to success, failure and pressure?
○ Are you feeling any pressure at the moment from home, school, health or whatever? If so, how are you dealing with it?
○ How do you feel about yourself right now?
○ Are there any areas in your life where you seem to keep getting into trouble?
○ How are you doing at school/college/work?
○ What kinds of hopes or visions do you have for the ways God might use you in the future?

Ready to lead

To think about:

○ Reflect on the roles that you play. Where do you think your identity comes from?
○ What things have you found useful in helping you stay close to God?

To do:

❍ Set aside some time during the week and, using the questions in the 'Wrapping it up' section, reflect on your relationship with God.

❍ Talk to an older Christian about what they do to stay close to God.

How's your heart?

Hey Ruth!

Sorry to contact you out of the blue like this, but I've got myself into a bit of a sticky situation and would love some advice.

A couple of days ago, some friends invited me to go for a drink at the pub with them. I didn't see a problem with it—I am 16, after all! But I knew my dad would think differently.

   The next morning, Dad asked me what I'd got up to the night before and I told him we'd gone to McDonald's. The problem is, one of the friends I went with came round this afternoon, and Dad asked them how they enjoyed their Big Mac. It took my friend a moment to work out what was going on, and I think Dad might have sussed that we weren't where I said we were.

I think I got away with it this time, but I'm aware that this sort of thing is starting to happen on a regular basis. Do you think it's a big issue?

Mmmmmm, how to respond?

What do you think? Would you suggest...

○ that they're straight with their dad about where they really were?
○ that they make sure, in future, they've brought their friend up to speed with the story?

○ that they reflect on why this kind of dishonesty is becoming a regular thing?

○ that they think through what they're going to do next time they get into this situation?

○ that they shouldn't worry about it—after all, it was only a little lie?

○ something else?

✳

Keep a close watch on how you live and on your teaching.
1 TIMOTHY 4:16

The Bible doesn't give us a specific list of pointers for how leaders should be chosen, but one thing is clear: God's leaders are to be chosen primarily on the strength of their character, not their abilities and skills. It would seem from the Bible that God chooses to develop the skills of people who are following him and are willing to be used by him.

In Chapter 1 we thought about some of the people that God chose to be leaders, and among them was King David. In his story, it was made clear that while people look at outward factors, such as how talented somebody is, or what they look like, or how much money they have, God uses a completely different way of measuring: he looks at what the heart is like.

Can you imagine how different life would be if that was the measure that people used? For instance, think of the time that so many children dread at school—the choosing of teams. They all know that the fastest, most able and most popular people are going to be picked first, while those who are not so fast—perhaps a bit clumsy—will be left until the very end. Imagine the difference if children were chosen because of their character. We might be surprised at the ones left standing!

But this is what God wants us to be clear about, and that's why I'm taking time to put this down as our second foundation for leadership. Christian leadership is not just about our knowledge, skills and talents;

it's mostly about our hearts, our character. God puts great emphasis on this. Throughout the Bible, he describes people more in terms of their character than in terms of their skills. When you read through the Old Testament books of Kings, it's fascinating to see how many kings are described as doing evil in the eyes of the Lord: their characters were not good.

Paul picks up on this issue in his letters to Timothy. He repeatedly refers to character traits that Timothy should be aiming to develop in himself and looking out for in others that he might choose for leadership. For example, Timothy himself should show:

○ constant faith in Christ and a clear conscience (1 Timothy 1:19)
○ godliness, being an example in lifestyle, love, faith and purity, and loving the Bible (4:7–13)
○ fairness in his dealings with people (no favouritism), and purity (5:21–22)
○ right living, faith, love, perseverance and gentleness (6:11)

When choosing other leaders, he should look for people who are beyond reproach, faithful in marriage, self-controlled, wise, of good reputation, hospitable, gentle, having integrity, being honest, having a clear conscience, and more besides! (3:1–13).

Paul even says that before church leaders are appointed, their lives should be closely examined for evidence of these qualities. In 1 Timothy 4:16, Paul sums this up for Timothy by saying, 'Keep a close watch on how you live and on your teaching.' In other words, make sure that the two match up so that you don't get caught out. Another word for this kind of consistency is 'integrity'. Integrity means checking that the words we speak match the actions of our lives.

On one occasion I'd been given the role of leading some children's work at a conference, and integrity was the subject. I racked my brains for days to think how to communicate this concept to a group of 5- to 9-year-olds, and I finally came up with an idea. I took the words from one storybook and the pictures from another and put the two together.

As I read the words from the first story, the pictures from the second story came up on a screen. I'd only read a few lines when a 5-year-old tapped me on the foot and whispered, 'You've got the wrong pictures!' He'd noticed very quickly. That's exactly what happens when we present one image with the words that we speak but the way that we live paints a very different picture.

Paul was aware that Timothy was a young leader and that older people might look down on him a bit. He encouraged Timothy not to let other people think less of him because he was young, but that actually his life should be an example to the other believers. I think Paul would say the same to us, too. We can be examples to other believers by the way that we live, through our faith and in the way we serve others. During my time as youth pastor, one of the most incredible things to observe was how parents were being influenced by their children. They could see their teenagers growing in faith and in commitment to God, and, for many parents and other adults in the church, it really challenged them about their own relationship with God.

Having integrity is also about being the same person no matter what situation or group of people we find ourselves in. I think school and college are two of the hardest places to live out our Christian faith, and sometimes it can feel as if we're one person when we're among our Christian friends and another person when we're with our school or college friends. Does this ring true for you? In Chapter 6 we'll look at this a bit more closely, but for now let's just register that God longs for us to have the confidence to be his person no matter who we're with—so that we grow in integrity and, in our school life as well as our church life, our words match our pictures.

Who you are when no one's looking

A well-known pastor and writer in America, Bill Hybels, has defined character as being 'who you are when no one's looking'.[6] Reputation is what people say that you are; character is what God knows that you are. Hybels believes that the world's most pressing need is to see people of good character. He goes on to say that in order to be people of good character, of godly character, we need to grow in the following areas:

○ Courage
○ Endurance
○ Love

Let's take a look at them one at a time.

Courage

Sometimes Christianity can be painted as the most boring thing on earth—no more than a dreary list of rules and regulations. But that was never God's plan. God is looking for people who will join in with the work that he's doing in the world. This work will change people's lives radically for the better; it will bring about justice for those suffering injustice; it will bring people into contact with the God who made them and loves them. When we respond to his invitation to follow him, we're responding to an invitation to join the most amazing adventure that we could ever know. That takes courage.

Courage isn't just about the brave, heroic acts that make it on to the *Ten O'Clock News*. Courage is about making the right choice in situations where we'd be tempted to compromise. Courage is about standing up for what is right, even when everyone else is saying something different. Courage is also about being prepared to follow wherever God may lead, even when we don't know how it's going to turn out.

As Bill Hybels says, 'Courage is foundational to being Christian... It takes courage to begin a walk with Christ, to reach out your hand and trust him. It takes courage to lead a life of obedience to Christ. It takes courage to be moral and build significant relationships with your... family and friends.'[7]

In the opening part of his second letter to Timothy, Paul reminds Timothy that he need not be afraid to do the work of God because 'God

41

has not given us a spirit of fear and timidity, but of power' (2 Timothy 1:7). God will give us the courage that we need in difficult situations, but we have to take that first step out into the unknown. Courage won't just come to us; we need to face whatever produces fear in us. Courageous people aren't those who were born without fear; they are ordinary people who refuse to let their fears stop them, and decide to trust God's promise.

Endurance

A few weeks ago, I was watching the London Marathon. According to those who have run it (a group that I don't find myself in!), at around the 20th mile something happens inside you, and you feel as if you can't carry on. Apparently it's called 'hitting the wall'. At that point, you have two choices. The first is to give in to those feelings and pull out of the race. The second is to muster every scrap of determination that you have and keep on running, despite the immense pain and your body screaming at you to stop.

In life, we come up against all sorts of situations where we feel like we've 'hit the wall' and the temptation to stop is very strong. Whether it's studying for exams, going to yet another trial for a hockey team, or auditioning once more for a part in a play, there often comes a point where we feel that we just can't do it again. Yet when we do, when we pick ourselves up one more time and keep on, refusing to give up, something happens to our character: we grow stronger and are able to face more and more.

If I was to run a marathon, my guess is that it wouldn't be at the 20th mile when I hit the wall. It would be at about the 20th metre! I'd need the sugar drink, and the blanket, and probably someone from St John Ambulance. But if I set my mind to it and, each time I went out training, ran just a bit further, it wouldn't be too long before I could go the whole distance.

It's the same in the Christian life. There may be times when it feels too hard. Our friends don't understand that we've chosen to follow God and might be very vocal about their feelings on the subject. The Bible reminds us, though, that there have been plenty of people who have gone ahead of us, who are cheering us on, encouraging us to get up one more time and keep on running.

The writer to the Hebrews wrote this to a group of Christians who were being persecuted for their faith:

Since we are surrounded by such a huge crowd of witnesses to the life of faith, let us strip off every weight that slows us down, especially the sin that so easily trips us up. And let us run with endurance the race God has set before us. We do this by keeping our eyes on Jesus, the champion who initiates and perfects our faith. Because of the joy awaiting him, he endured the cross, disregarding its shame. Now he is seated in the place of honour beside God's throne. (Hebrews 12:1–2)

This writer reminds us that Jesus had the most difficult challenge to face—death on the cross—yet he kept going because he knew the reward that was waiting for him: he knew that, through his death, all people could come to know God.

In those times when we want to give up, we should remember the crowd of witnesses cheering us on, encouraging us to make the right choice or to keep going when it's hard. And we should remember the promise of God that he will give his Holy Spirit so that we are never alone (John 14:18).

Love

We have a real problem in the English language with the word 'love'—because we only have the one word. We have to use the same word to say that we love custard and that we love our family. The other problem is that we can tend to think of 'love' as a gushy thing, mostly for girls. However, the Bible's understanding of the word 'love' is not remotely gushy or girly. In the Bible, love is often costly and, as followers of Jesus, we are asked to truly love people—all people, including those we would consider to be our friends and those we wouldn't.

In John 15, Jesus says that the mark of love is that we'd be willing to lay down our life for our friends (v. 13). That sounds pretty costly to me. Yet the challenge, I find, is not so much about being prepared to die for my friends or the people around me; it's more about being prepared to inconvenience myself for them. It means taking the time to be friendly to the people who always seem to be on the edge of things. It means asking my elderly neighbour if there's any shopping I can do for them, or being willing to forgive people who have hurt me, or having compassion for people who are suffering.

If we want to be people of good, godly character, this is the kind of love that is required.

Self-help or God's transformation?

The great news is that we're not left on our own to grow this kind of character. The reality is that we would never manage it. There are so many self-help books in bookshops and libraries, mostly of the *Ten Easy Steps to Fix Your Life* variety. But character growth takes time and is unlikely to happen in ten easy steps.

God asks us to look at our lives and honestly ask ourselves what the areas are in which we need to grow. What are the areas where we seem to get tripped up? Paul mentions three qualities in 1 Timothy 4: love, faith and purity. It's not clear whether Paul highlighted these because Timothy needed to work on them particularly or whether he was just pulling three character traits out of the air as an example, but they are helpful for us all to think about.

When it all goes wrong

One of the things I love most about the Bible is that it doesn't include just stories of perfect people who got it right all the time. In fact, most of the characters we come across made some terrible mistakes in their lives, yet God continued to use them.

Let's think about King David, whom God described as 'a man after my own heart' (see 1 Samuel 13:14). It's easy to read something like that and assume that David must have been perfect, living in perfect harmony with God every day of his life. But as we read through his biography we come across episodes that he would probably prefer we didn't know about. There was one time in particular when David's army was away at war and, rather than going with his soldiers, he decided to stay at home. We're told that as he was wandering around on the roof of the palace, he noticed one of his neighbours having a bath. Did I mention that she was beautiful and could easily have won the Miss Israel competition? Well, David couldn't look away, and became so fixated by her that we then read a story of adultery, which then to David arranging the death of the woman's soldier husband on the battlefield. (You can read the story in 2 Samuel 11.)

It was not his greatest moment, you might say. God sent a prophet to confront David about what he'd done, and this is where the vital moment in the story occurs. With his power, David could have arranged for the prophet to be dealt with as well, but we're told that he was completely devastated when he confronted the reality of what he had done (2 Samuel 12). Psalm 51 is his prayer of repentance, acknowledging to God how badly he had got things wrong and asking God to forgive him and to restore their relationship.

Now, it's not that God doesn't take these matters seriously. He really does. But his promise is that his forgiveness is always available for those who are truly sorry for wrong things said or done. God recognizes that we will make mistakes, but he wants to know if we're ready to get up again, turn around from the wrong direction in which we've been heading and come back to him. Then his forgiveness is waiting for us.

There have been times in my own story when I know I got it badly wrong. There was one period in particular when I felt as if I'd blown it completely. I spent weeks wallowing in misery because I couldn't believe that God would want to use me any more. I eventually talked to a friend about what had happened, and my friend was great, reminding me of God's promise to forgive and restore, without excusing what I'd done.

God did that for David. Jesus did it for his disciple Peter after Peter had denied even knowing him, he does it with me and he'll do it for you. Letting God down does not mark the end of your leadership role; staying down is what will do that. God longs for us to know how much he loves us, and he has done everything possible so that we can be made right with him and go on sharing in his kingdom work, being made more and more like Jesus.

Wrapping it up

God's promise to us is that, as we become aware of areas of our character that need to change, and as we talk to him about them, he will be at work in us, making us more like Jesus. The Bible is full of people whose lives were changed through their encounter with Jesus:

○ **Zacchaeus:** transformed from a greedy and dishonest man to a generous man (Luke 19:2, 8).
○ **The woman at the well:** transformed from a participant in wrong relationships to the first evangelist to the Samaritan people (John 4:18, 29).
○ **Saul:** transformed from a persecutor of Christians to a persecuted Christian (Acts 9:3, 15–16).
○ **Thomas:** transformed from a doubter to a believer (John 20:25–28).
○ **Peter:** transformed from a coward to the most courageous church planter (John 18:17; 21:17).
○ **Lazarus:** transformed from being dead to being alive! (John 11:38–44).

The list goes on. There is nothing and no one beyond God's ability to transform. That is what he loves to do, and that is what he has promised to do. He cares deeply about our character, for our own sake but also for the sake of the people we will lead. We will never achieve greatness as a leader if we haven't allowed God to mould our character.

Ready to lead

To think about:

○ As you think about your character, what are the areas where you'd like God's help?

○ What do you think Paul would say to you as a young leader?

To do:

○ Read John 15:1–17 during the coming week and ask God to speak to you through it.

○ Ask someone that you know and trust what they think your strongest character traits are.

Knowing your make-up

Dear Ruth

Thanks for the card you sent. I still can't believe that I've been made head girl!

It's not usually me in my family that gets recognized for things. You know what they're like—Matthew with his incredible sporting talent, and Sally with her incredible musical gift, and me stuck in the middle, not quite sure what I'm good at or what I can do.

You were a middle child too, weren't you? Did you ever feel like that? It seems that it's so obvious what they're good at, but I don't think there's anything in particular for me. I'm just OK at things.

I always thought my shyness would stop me being able to be head girl, but it seems not. I'm not quite sure why I've been chosen but really glad that I have!

See you soon.

Mmmmmm, how to respond?

What do you think? Would you suggest...

○ that there's more to her than she thinks, and tell her what you think her skills are?

○ that she should just accept that her siblings are more gifted than she is?

○ that she asks other friends what they think she's good at?
○ that this may be a jealousy issue?
○ that she should give thanks for the way in which God has made her and others, and celebrate both?
○ something else?

✳

Fan into flames the spiritual gift God gave you when I laid my hands on you.
2 TIMOTHY 1:6

I have to confess to being something of a people watcher. I particularly like spending time in airport restaurants (when I haven't overslept!) and watching as people pass by, wondering who they are, what they do and where they're off to. I find them endlessly fascinating.

Don't you think it's amazing that you never find two people who are exactly the same? Even identical twins have differences in personality and skills. When I think of my own family, the differences there are huge. If you were to put my sister and brother and me in a room full of people, I doubt very much that you could guess we were related. We look so very different and we are such different personalities that even if you spent time with us, there wouldn't be much to give away the family connection. In terms of what we enjoy or are good at, again the differences are vast. Yet we've all been brought up by the same parents in the same home.

A while ago, some friends bought me a book called The Ark, which is a beautifully illustrated commentary on creation. In it the artist muses on the idea that when God was creating all the animals, it was as if he went into a storeroom and looked at the massive range of materials on offer (tiger print, fur, spots and so on) and all the different ideas for parts of the body (long neck, short legs, big ears and so on), and just had the most fun time putting them together in a million creative ways.[8]

As we look at the world, it's not hard to see the hand of a creator

God, yet the Bible tells us that when God made people, they were the pinnacle of his creation. While he proclaimed that all the previous parts of creation were 'good', when he looked at the human beings, he was able to announce that all he had made was 'very good' (Genesis 1:31).

In Ephesians 2:10, Paul expresses it like this: 'We are God's masterpiece. He has created us anew in Christ Jesus, so we can do the good things he planned for us long ago.' God's masterpiece! His work of art! You and I are one-off originals, and we are created by God with a purpose.

I hear so many motivational talks given to students that go along the lines of 'You can be anything that you want to be. If you set your mind to it, you can do whatever you want.' Now that's great and, no doubt, highly motivating, but something always feels uneasy inside me when I hear statements like that. I wonder, 'Is that true? Can we really be whatever we want to be?' I think the answer is actually 'no', not if we believe that we're uniquely made. However, can I be everything that God created me to be? Most definitely, yes!

Did you spot the bit in Ephesians 2:10 where Paul says that there are things God has planned for us to do, good things that we can contribute because of the way in which he has made us? God is looking for ordinary people who will use all that he has given to them in the way that he's created them, to be part of his kingdom work.

Rick Warren says, 'Instead of trying to reshape yourself to be like someone else, you should celebrate the shape God has given you.'[9] It's very easy for us to spend a lot of our life wishing we were like someone else, and not seeing the amazing way in which God has put us together, with our interests, our abilities and our personality, along with the unique experiences that our lives have held, and the way in which he wants to use those attributes. It's also very easy to imagine that God only uses adults to make a difference in the world, but that is completely untrue. Through the generations, God has used children and young people to make a difference in their homes, schools, churches, communities and the wider world.

God has signed his name to you, just as an artist signs their work, and he's given us a choice to be either a contributor or a consumer—to use the gifts and skills he's given us to serve others, or to sit back and let others serve us. Everyone has a contribution to make—God planned it that way.

So how do we discover the 'shape' that God has given us? A helpful way of looking at this is to take each letter of the word 'shape' and look at a different characteristic that is evident in our lives, to create a bigger picture of who we are and the gifts and skills that we have. (This is a model that has been developed by Erik Rees, pastor of the Ministry and S.H.A.P.E. Discovery teams at Saddleback Church in the USA.)

○ S stands for 'Spiritual gifts', those special gifts that God gives to his people.
○ H stands for 'Heart', those things that you care deeply about.
○ A stands for 'Abilities', the natural talents that you have.
○ P stands for 'Personality', the way in which you are wired.
○ E stands for 'Experience', the collection of stuff from your past that God wants to use for others' futures.

Spiritual gifts

This is what the Bible says about spiritual gifts:

God has given gifts to each of you from his great variety of spiritual gifts. Manage them well so that God's generosity can flow through you. Are you called to be a speaker? Then speak as though God himself were speaking through you. Are you called to help others? Do it with all the strength and energy that God supplies. (1 Peter 4:10–11, NLT, 1996)

Spiritual gifts are gifts that God gives to his people to help the Church be all that the Church is meant to be. God doesn't give these gifts so that people can feel proud about their special abilities, or, as my friend puts it, as 'trophies for the mantelpiece'. Rather, he gives them as tools for the job of 'building the body', building up his Church, so that we may witness in the world.

In the New Testament you will find a number of lists of these gifts. Here are some of the main ones:

Romans 12:6-8

❍ Exhortation/encouragement
❍ Giving
❍ Helps
❍ Mercy
❍ Prophecy
❍ Leadership
❍ Teaching

1 Corinthians 12:8-10, 28

❍ Administration
❍ Discerning spirits
❍ Faith
❍ Healing
❍ Helps
❍ Interpretation of tongues
❍ Knowledge
❍ Miracles
❍ Prophecy
❍ Speaking in tongues
❍ Wisdom

Ephesians 4:11

❍ Apostle
❍ Teacher
❍ Prophet

○ Evangelist
○ Pastor

The difference between spiritual gifts and what we would call 'talents' is that spiritual gifts are given by God, and only to Christians, because the point of spiritual gifts is that they must always be used for the sake of his kingdom.

You may already be aware of the spiritual gifts that God has given you, or you might not yet be sure what your gifts are. Remember that he gives different gifts to different people at different times. If you are a Christian, he has definitely given you some. In Appendix 1, at the back of this book, I've provided a list of the spiritual gifts, along with a short description of each one. You might like to work through that list and ask yourself whether:

○ this is definitely your gift.
○ this is possibly your gift.
○ you're unsure whether this is your gift or not.
○ this is definitely not your gift.

You could also ask someone else to suggest what they think your gifts are.

This is important, so let me repeat it: God has given all of us, as his people, gifts. Occasionally they may emerge fully developed but, more often than not, they work in the same way as our other talents: we have to use them in order for them to grow and for us to become more skilled in their use. As you read down the list of gifts, there may be some that you know you haven't got but would like to see developed in your life. God is very open to us asking for particular gifts, particularly when it's to meet a need that we see around us.

No one person has all the spiritual gifts, which again is a reminder that we need to work alongside others. If everyone had all the gifts, we'd no longer see the point in working together to build up the Church.

I love spending time with my youth group, and particularly enjoy seeing how they are growing in their gifts. Jo most definitely has the gift of encouragement. Every Thursday evening, when we meet, she spends most of the evening going round the group, chatting to each person individually, asking how their week has been and encouraging them in whatever they're doing. Tim has just recently started leading worship in our evening service. He writes his own songs and loves to use his musical gift to lead others. Stephen has the gift of being an evangelist. Every week he's planning some event at school that he can invite his friends to, and sharing his faith with others comes very naturally to him. I could go on, but at this point you might like to think of friends in your group, if you're part of one, and what gifts they might have. You could also develop the gift of encouragement and say something to them about what you've seen in them.

Heart

I've just finished reading an autobiography by Kay Warren (wife of Rick). Kay describes herself as an average American woman who had spent most of her life just getting on with the business of family life—until one morning in 2002.

The day had started like any other day, and, finding herself with some time to spare, she picked up a magazine from her coffee table. As she flicked through the magazine, her eye was caught by an article on AIDS orphans in Africa. This was not a new subject to her, as she'd been aware for years about the AIDS pandemic, yet on this occasion it was like reading about it for the first time. Her heart broke as she read about the 12 million children who had been orphaned because of the disease, and her life has never been the same since. Today she splits her time between visiting places that are ravaged by HIV/Aids, offering support and teaching around the world on the subject, encouraging others to see the part they can play in alleviating this devastating disease.

I have a friend who, after a short-term mission trip to Thailand, was so appalled by the conditions under which children with disabilities were made to live, abandoned and rejected and with no hope of reaching their potential, that she changed the whole direction of her life. Nicola came back to the UK, researched different programmes and then returned to Thailand to set up a development project called '1 Step, 2 Step' for children with cerebral palsy. The issue had taken hold of her heart and she had to do something about it.

Because we have been created by God, he has left his clues inside us about how he wants to use us. For each of us, the story or issue that takes hold of our hearts will be different. But God asks us to listen to our hearts and respond to the nudges that we feel. By asking ourselves some questions we can get a clearer picture of what we're passionate about, the things that really take hold of our hearts.

○ What are the areas of life where you would love to make a difference?
○ If you could do anything at all, and it was guaranteed to succeed and your friends and family fully supported you in it, what would you do?
○ What issues or situations in your school, town, country or world get you so exasperated that you feel you have to take action?

These are the things that you are passionate about. If you're not sure how to answer these questions, don't worry. Now is a great time to be discovering what God wants to put on your heart, to make a difference.

You may find that you're passionate about a whole range of stuff, as well as causes that you encounter. You may be passionate about music or sports or design. We need to listen to ourselves about these things, too, because my experience tells me that God tends to use us in areas that we're passionate about.

Abilities

Apparently I didn't speak until I was quite old (in developmental terms, I mean—it's not as if I was 15!) Then, one day, I opened my mouth and started to speak pretty much perfectly. My friends and family will tell you that, since that moment, I haven't really stopped talking—and today quite a lot of my job revolves around that ability!

Singing is a different matter, however. I remember that one of my most humiliating moments at primary school was auditioning for the school choir. I was the only child who auditioned who didn't get in. I must have been bad, because I think at primary school they have to accept pretty much anyone. To make matters worse, singing was one of my sister's greatest talents. I was devastated.

We touched on abilities in Chapter 1, but, in case you've forgotten what we said, let me remind you that our abilities, or talents, are those things that we can just naturally do and, in fact, can't help ourselves doing. All human beings have talents, and most of our talents will be formed by the time we're an adult.

So how do we find out what our abilities are? Ask yourself the question, 'What do I love doing, that comes fairly naturally and easily to me?' Do you love to be out on the sports field? Do you enjoy being creative, either in thought or in design? Are you musically talented? Do maths problems fill you with delight? Can you organize for Britain? Do you have the knack of motivating those around you? Do you think nothing of cooking for 20?

These are all natural abilities. God's intention is that we link them with our spiritual gifts and get inspired by our passion to do something that demonstrates his creativity and goodness to the world around us.

Personality

There is no such thing as a good personality or a bad personality. We can be people of good or bad character, but personality is a different thing. Our character is something that we can work at changing, with God's help, but our personality is pretty much given and formed by the time we're four or five. That's quite incredible, isn't it?

While passion will help us work out the 'where' of using our spiritual gifts and abilities, understanding our personality will go a long way to helping us work out how we will use our gifts and abilities. Our personality affects the way in which we do just about everything, from making decisions, handling difficult situations or approaching new people to whether we're more likely to approach a situation competitively or cooperatively.

Today there are loads of different tests that we can do to find out our personality type. They are helpful to a certain degree, although they can sometimes end up putting us in boxes, or providing us with great excuses for bad behaviour. 'That's just the way I am' is a well-worn phrase used to explain things away!

However, there are some important lessons that we can learn about ourselves from the way we respond to people and to different opportunities, which will give us a clue to how we might go about using our gifts and abilities.

Some of us are more outgoing and love to be surrounded by loads of people. Others of us prefer to have a few close friends. Some of us love being the centre of attention, while others are far happier behind the scenes. Some of us love working in a team with other people, while others see every task as a competition. Some of us will tell anyone anything and everything about our lives—how we're feeling, what's upsetting us, and so on—whereas others keep far more to themselves.

There is no right or wrong; being one way is not better than being another way. We're just different. And that's good news. If we were all raving extraverts, constantly wanting the limelight, so many people would get overlooked. What's important is that we recognize how we're made so that we can look for opportunities that are suited to our personality. That doesn't mean we never step out of our comfort zone, but it does mean that we know where we work best.

On meeting me, most people assume that I'm an extravert. I spend a lot of my time speaking to large crowds of people, and I love to be in the middle of busy situations. But I'm actually an introvert. I love being around people, but I need to make sure that I have a certain amount of time on my own. That's where I recoup my energy. It's important that I'm aware of this, because I have to build that time alone into my life, otherwise I find myself in an exhausted state, completely 'peopled out'.

Experiences

The final element that makes up our 'shape' is our experiences, both the good ones and the bad. The person we are today has been moulded by the experiences we've gone through. Sometimes it's hard to understand how the difficulties that we've faced can ever be used for good, but they can. I'm amazed at how often God brings people across my path who are going through something that I've experienced. In those moments, I'm able to come alongside them, empathize with them and encourage them to believe that life will get better. And that is what God will do with every experience that you've been through. Nothing will be wasted if you are willing to share it carefully with the people God brings across your path.

So, when we pull all these things together, we have a clearer idea of how God has made us. The question then is, 'With all that I am and all that I've been through, what can I do to make a difference in this world?' God's intention is that you use the person that you are, the gifts and abilities that you have, to honour him.

I love the story of the Scottish athlete Eric Liddell. You may have seen his story, told in the film *Chariots of Fire* (a bit dated now, but still an inspiring film). Liddell was a Christian, training to be a missionary in China, but he was also a great athlete. One of my favourite scenes from the film is where Eric is walking with his sister, Jenny, in the countryside. At this point, he is explaining or, to be more accurate, defending to Jenny the amount of time he spends running. She feels that he should be doing more preaching and committing more time to leading the people in their church. In a way, it feels as if Jenny is questioning Eric's faith and his commitment to being a missionary. After a lengthy discussion, Eric responds, 'Jenny, you've got to understand. I believe God made me for a purpose—for China. But he also made me fast, and when I run, I feel his pleasure.' Eric was selected for the 1924 Olympic Games in Paris to compete in the 100 metres race. However, this event was scheduled for a Sunday, and Liddell felt that he would be dishonouring God if he competed on that day. So he ran instead in the 400 metres event, scheduled for the Tuesday, and won the race in a new world-record time of 47.6 seconds.

Running was a natural ability that Eric believed God had given him, which wasn't separate from what we might consider the more 'spiritual' aspects of his life. In using his running ability, he honoured God, because that was a talent that God had given him. We can know, too, that God has made us as we are, for a purpose. That same God has given us different loves and abilities—to run, or build, or write, or act. God wants you, like Eric Liddell, to live for his purpose, and he wants you to feel his pleasure.

As we finish this chapter, let's return to Paul and Timothy. Paul recognized that Timothy had spiritual gifts and abilities, and his longing for Timothy was that he should use what God had given him in his leadership role. He tells Timothy that he must not just settle with his gifts and abilities as they are; rather, he must 'fan into flame' those gifts (2 Timothy 1:6). What a great phrase! Paul wants Timothy to realize that God gives us gifts and abilities but we have a responsibility, too, to take every opportunity to use them so that they can get better and better, and so that we can be more effective as the unique person that God has created us to be.

Mike Pilavachi tells the story of a young guy in his youth group who was desperate to lead worship. Each week he would come along with his guitar and attempt to play worship songs for the group. Apparently the first few months were pretty painful, as he was incredibly enthusiastic but not that proficient. He persisted, though, and Mike continued to give him opportunities, and gradually he improved. That young guy was Matt Redman. It's easy to think that he's always been the great musician and singer/songwriter that he is today. But we would never have known of his gifts if he hadn't persisted in 'fanning into flame' his gifts, and responding to the opportunities given to him.

Wrapping it up

If you feel that you've a long way to go, please don't give up. Continue to fan into flame your gifts. Look for opportunities to grow, to use your gift alongside others who are maybe a little bit ahead of you—learn from them and see how God will keep his side of the commitment.

Ready to lead

To think about:

○ 'With all that I am and all that I've been through, what can I do to make a difference in the world?' What would be your response?

○ What can you do to 'fan into flame' the gifts that you have?

To do:

○ Spend some time thinking about your SHAPE, and write down what you think are your particular talents, gifts, personality and experience:

S _____

_____

H _____

_____

A _____

_____

P _____

_____

E _____

_____

○ Think about a friend—the gifts they have and the person they are. Can you do something to encourage them?

5

Part of the team

Hi!

Thanks so much for dropping your tent off for me—can't believe that Soul Survivor is only two weeks away!

There's about 18 of us going so it should be a laugh—that's if we ever make it there! Seriously, it looks like that could be a bit of an issue. As you know, Ben is heading up the trip and is responsible for organizing it, but he's been completely hopeless. First of all, he lost all of our parents' consent forms so we had to get them done again, then he booked us in for the wrong week.

I'm part of the team that he's put together for when we're there—sorting out cooking rotas, and arranging who's in with who and that kind of stuff. But I'm wondering whether I should actually take over the leadership of the trip now.

What do you think?

Mmmmmm, how to respond?

What do you think? Would you suggest...

○ that they just take charge—it's so much easier that way?
○ that they ask Ben if there's anything they can help with before the group gets to Soul Survivor?

○ that they just get on and do everything he asks them to do, with a good attitude and to the best of their ability?

○ that they make sure everyone is aware of how rubbish Ben has been?

○ that they think of Ben's positive attributes and praise him for those?

○ something else?

Having laid the foundations of establishing that Christian leadership is about servanthood, recognizing that a Christian leader is, above all, a follower of Christ, and identifying that good character is of primary importance to God, it's now time to move on and look at some of the practical aspects of leadership.

Some of the best experiences in my life have involved working as part of a team. There is something uniquely special about working together towards an established aim. Leadership in the Bible is almost always seen as a team thing, and there are a number of reasons for this.

Firstly, right at the start, God said that it was not good for people to be alone. That's why he created Eve to be alongside Adam to look after the earth (Genesis 2:18, 22). Secondly, it's a biblical principle that people are in a much better situation if they have others alongside them:

Two people are better off than one, for they can help each other succeed. If one person falls, the other can reach out and help. But someone who falls alone is in real trouble. Likewise, two people lying close together can keep each other warm. But how can one be warm alone? A person standing alone can be attacked and defeated, but two can stand back-to-back and conquer. Three are even better, for a triple-braided cord is not easily broken. (Ecclesiastes 4:9–12)

Thirdly, as Christian leaders, we're meant to model something of what it means to be church. The image most often used in the New Testament for the church is that of a body (in other words, it is made up of more than one part), and the reason why this image is used is that God himself is a team, made up of Father, Son and Holy Spirit.

Jesus himself chose to bring others alongside him rather than going it alone in his ministry, so this in itself provides us with a good biblical model for working as a team.

There are also some really practical reasons for working in teams.

○ One person alone won't have all the necessary skills to accomplish what needs to be done. We need each other's gifts and skills.
○ One person alone won't have all the wisdom needed to lead.
○ It's much more fun to work with other people, and leadership doesn't feel like such a huge weight of responsibility if it's shared among a number of people.

Supporting those in leadership

One of the key roles that we can play as we grow in leadership, and as established leaders, is to support those who are leading us. We won't always be the team leader, and it's important that we also know how to be a good team player. There are a number of ways in which we can do this.

Getting on board with their vision

Depending on the nature of the team that you're part of, there will be different goals in mind. Obviously, if you're part of a football team, then the captain's aim is very clear—winning! In other teams the aims can seem less obvious. It's worth taking time to understand what the team leader's aims are for the team, and how we can best use our gifts and skills to work towards achieving that aim. If we don't understand what the aim is, we can end up undermining the work that's going on. For example, if you're part of a children's ministry team, the overall leader's aim may be to introduce children to God and the Bible in a fun and caring environment, so as a team member you might use your gifts to help create a loving and happy atmosphere.

Being an encourager

It took me quite a while to realize that those in leadership over me needed encouragement as much as I did. The writer to the Hebrews says this to his readers: 'Remember your leaders who taught you the word of God. Think of all the good that has come from their lives, and follow the example of their faith' (13:7). THE MESSAGE translates 'remember' as 'appreciate', which is really at the heart of what the writer was saying. Appreciate them, encourage them, let them know that you value their work on your behalf. Why? Because they are people like you and me, who are strengthened by positive comments from others. Often, our default position can be to criticize our leaders, so making it a discipline to think positively rather than negatively is the mark of a good team player with good character.

Influencing others

As you may well have experienced, it can be hard work leading a team of human beings with different personalities. As a team player, we can be someone who encourages and influences others to play their part well through our example, making the overall leader's role slightly easier. Remember the passage we looked at in Chapter 3 about being an example to the believers? Well, it counts here, too.

This isn't about being a 'Goody Two-Shoes'; it's about taking leadership seriously and supporting those who are leading us.

Members of the team

Within any team you will find a number of different personalities. Here are a few that you may encounter:

○ **Distracted Dave:** nice guy but finds it very hard to stay focused on the job in hand.

○ **Can-do Kate:** a 'nothing's a problem' kind of person, always ready with a solution to any difficulty. Highly positive outlook on life, the world and the universe. Motivates others to get involved and make things happen.

○ **Negative Neil:** always the first to tell you why something won't work, or how the team tried a particular approach 20 years ago and it didn't work then, so it won't work now.

○ **Task-focused Tom:** very clear about what the team is here to do, but sometimes forgets that the team is made up of people who need caring for, encouraging and developing.

○ **Talkative Terry:** often a positive member of the team, but sometimes doesn't know when to keep quiet and let others participate. Doesn't really need anybody else for a conversation because he has so much to say himself.

○ **Dependable Dan:** can be counted on completely to do what he says he will do. Will always be on time and ready for anything.

○ **Gossiping Gaynor:** highly suspicious of the rest of the team and enjoys a good gossip behind their backs, spreading rumours that may or may not be true but are generally not very helpful.

○ **Encouraging Eric:** loves to praise others for the things that they're doing, and always notices achievements that people have made. Constantly looks for the good in people and comments on it.

○ **Fun Fiona:** committed to the task but also believes that fun is a high priority. Looks for ways of celebrating good things that are happening, and lifts the atmosphere in any situation.

○ **Critical Claire:** a bit like Negative Neil, but focuses more on the faults of individuals rather than pulling apart ideas.

○ **Caring Cassie:** cares far more about the people on the team than the task of the team. Likes to make sure that everyone is OK and happy. A great person to have around but sometimes needs to be reminded that there is also a job to do.

I admit that these are caricatures of people, but I'm sure there are individuals that you recognize here, and you may even recognize yourself. Being a good team player is a discipline. We have a choice about how we behave and respond as team members, and how we support those in the overall leader position. We can either be someone who works to build the team up or be someone who pulls it apart.

I'm so grateful for the people in the teams I have led who have chosen to come with a 'can-do' mentality. They have been willing to do whatever it takes to fulfil the aims of the team, not worrying about whether they are the centre of attention or not. As Doug Fields, an American youth pastor, says, 'Leaders are known for how they react in adverse situations, not for their ability to be in the spotlight.'[10]

In the work team that I'm part of, we have a commitment to each other that:

○ rather than being cynical and negative, we will practise being thankful.
○ rather than being critical, we will be people who love and look for the best in others.
○ rather than being gossips, we will be committed to speaking the truth.

These may seem like insignificant points, but the difference they make is quite dramatic.

Faithful in the small things

In Chapter 2, I mentioned the advice that I was given about leadership—that it involves a lot of chair moving. This is a good way of identifying those who really want to grow as leaders. When I'm seeking leaders to take on more responsible roles, I'll always look out for those who've been quietly willing to carry out the less glamorous jobs, those who turn up early to get the meeting set up, and those who stay late to clear everything away. There are a lot of people who enjoy doing the 'visible' stuff, but the crowd thins out when it comes to the seemingly insignificant jobs. The biblical pattern that Jesus sets is that those who show themselves to be responsible in the small things will be the ones who go on to be given greater responsibility.

When I was just beginning in leadership, I had great dreams about what I'd love to do for God, but it felt as if the day was years away when all those things could be possible. Then I heard the following words, spoken by Leighton Ford on the Arrow *Growing Leaders* course. I stuck them on my wall and used them as a prayer that God would bring to fulfilment the dreams that I believed he'd given me, but that he'd also help me to stay faithful in doing the small things.

If you want to be a leader in the kingdom of God, never lose sight of the greatest dream God has given you, but don't despise the day of small beginnings.

If we prove ourselves to be faithful as team players, supporting someone else in their leadership and vision, God will honour us and move us into positions of more responsibility.

Now, you may be wondering how all this relates to teams outside the church situation. Well, I hope you will see that it does connect. As I outlined in Chapter 1, you are a Christian leader no matter where you are, because you are a Christian. God's intention is that wherever you find yourself in leadership or as part of a team, you act according to his principles so that others can see in you something of what he's like.

When things go wrong

Being part of a team is often brilliant and a lot of fun. At times, however, situations can get tense and conflict can arise. Conflict is not necessarily bad. When you have a number of different personalities working together, there are bound to be times when disagreement happens. What matters is how we handle it. Conflict may take a number of different forms:

○ A difference in opinion about how something should be done.
○ Upset or offence caused by the behaviour of a fellow team member.
○ Disagreement with a decision that the team leader has made.

Let's take a look at how you might handle each of these situations in turn. People will tend to handle the first situation in different ways according to personality type and how much they dislike engaging in conflict.

Denial: This is the ostrich approach, where you put your head in the sand and hope that the situation will just go away or resolve itself.

Compromise: You try to find some sort of middle ground, where you give up some of your views, and others give up some of theirs.

Direction: You make the decision and insist that it's done that way, despite what others may think.

Surrender: You allow others to have their way entirely.

Agreement: You work through to finding a solution that sounds good to all involved.

The key thing in this situation is not to let it get personal. The ideas you're talking about are separate from the people involved. Just because someone disagrees with one of your ideas, it does not mean they're criticizing you as a person. It's important to keep that in mind.

The Bible provides us with a very clear way of handling the kind of disagreement between team members found in the second scenario. In Matthew 18:15–17, Jesus' advice is that first you go and talk with the person in private about what they have done or said to upset you. If they refuse to listen, or refuse to resolve the situation, take someone else with you next time so that there is a witness to what's going on. If the person still refuses to listen, it's up to the leaders to take some disciplinary action. The hope is, though, that the situation will be resolved in the first instance. However, it does take courage to try to talk conflict through. That's why it's one of the key character traits of a leader.

For the third situation, there are again a few ways in which you could approach it. You might simply make up your mind that, even though you disagree with the decision, you will go along with it to support the leader. Or you could reflect on why you feel so strongly about the decision and chat through your thoughts with the leader, perhaps making some alternative suggestions. Finally, if you really can't find any way to support the leader's decision, you may need to step down from the team.

Leading the team

You may already find yourself in the position of team leader. If so, there are some issues that you can think about to make you even more effective in your role. In every team there are three 'needs' that the team leader needs to be aware of:

○ **The need to achieve a common task:** as we saw in Chapter 1, leaders help people to achieve God's goals. For example, a leader of a small group ought to know why the group exists, and be equipped to help the group achieve its goals. The same applies to a children's group leader or a netball team leader—in fact, to any leader.
○ **The need to be held together:** any team requires a feeling of unity, enabling its members to do far more together than they could do on their own. It's your role as team leader to find ways of doing this— creating times of celebration, helping team members get to know each other and so on.
○ **The needs of the individual:** each person in a team comes with specific personal needs. These needs are various, they change, and they are sometimes known and sometimes unknown. As team leader, your role is to be aware of the different individuals in your team. What are their strengths and what are their weaknesses? How do they need to be encouraged? What can you do to get to know them better and help them feel more part of the team?

When these three factors come together, you have a really strong team.

Before we move on, let's take a moment to think more specifically about what it means to be a leader in a non-church context. I'm really hoping that some of you reading this are in leadership positions in your school, or perhaps captains of sports teams. You have a crucial role to play as a leader, because God's intention for you is that you will be an ambassador for him. As you're probably aware, an ambassador is someone who represents their country to another country. As Christian leaders, we are ambassadors for the kingdom of God. As people look at the way we behave and act towards others, they will be learning a lot about what we believe.

For leaders in those non-church situations, all that we've talked about in previous chapters holds true. As you lead there, you should aim to serve the people in your team, and to develop your skills and gifts in that context, asking God to help your character to become more like that of Christ so that under your leadership people will be able to glimpse a different way of living.

Wrapping it up

When teams work well, they are the best things on earth. As growing leaders, we have a responsibility to play our role on the team to the best of our ability and with our best attitude.

Here's Paul talking to the church at Philippi about Timothy:

If the Lord is willing, I hope to send Timothy to you soon for a visit... You know how Timothy has proved himself. Like a son with his father, he has served with me in preaching the Good News.
PHILIPPIANS 2:19, 22

We're told in Acts 16:1–3 that Paul first met Timothy in a place called Lystra, and, because of the great reputation that Timothy had among the believers, Paul decided that he wanted him as part of his team. A few years on, Paul is able to write to one of his favourite churches that he's going to send Timothy to them, because he knows that he will be a real encouragement to them, as he has been to Paul.

Wouldn't it be great if people looked at us in that way? Imagine if they saw how willing we were to serve with a good attitude: their instant reaction would be, 'I want you on my team.'

Again, this is another opportunity to be an example to those around us, to imprint ourselves on them.

Ready to lead

To think about:

❍ If you can, think of two teams that you've been part of. What made them work well, or maybe not so well?

❍ What one lesson have you learnt from this chapter that will help you be a better team player/leader?

To do:

❍ Think of a leader that you can encourage this week. Maybe you could write them a quick note to let them know you appreciate them.

❍ Do something over the next couple of weeks that will help you to get to know a team-mate better.

6

Leading where you are

Hi Ruth

Sorry I wasn't very chatty on Friday at youth group. It wasn't anything to do with the group or what was happening there, but thanks for asking if it was.

Well, actually, I guess it is something to do with youth group. I love being part of that group, and I know that through it I'm really growing as a Christian. God has taught me so much there over these last months. So why am I so unhappy?

I think the problem is that I know that's not the whole picture of who I am. At school I'm surprised to find myself as one of the popular gang. It's not something that I've tried to do, but these people are my friends and I don't want to lose them.

The thing is, if they knew I was a Christian I'm not sure how they'd respond.

I love being at youth group, and I'm loving being part of this group of friends, but I sometimes wonder if I'm living a double life.

Mmmmmm, how to respond?

What do you think? Would you suggest...

○ that they invite their school friends along to the next Bible study at church?
○ that they give up their school friends and just hang around with Christian friends?
○ that they continue living a double life—it's not that much of a problem?
○ that they find another Christian at school that they can talk to and pray with about this?
○ that they find a way of bringing their two lives together?
○ something else?

*

In February 1994, news broke of one of the most damaging spy cases in US history. Aldrich Ames was an American CIA agent, and was actually the head of the CIA's Soviet operations, an incredibly high-ranking position. However, everything started to come undone for this agent as it emerged that not only was he working for the CIA, he was also working for the KGB, selling America's secrets to the Soviet Union and then Russia. He was operating as a double agent. In April 1994, he was sentenced to life imprisonment without parole for his actions. His final statement included this sentence: 'No punishment by this court can balance or ease the profound shame and guilt I bear.'

The role of double agent has always fascinated me. How can someone get away with living two lives? How can someone enjoy living two lives, with the constant knowledge that they are deceiving and betraying people who have trusted them?

Then it dawned on me. I, too, had spent a number of years living as a double agent. In my early teenage years, when I was at church among my Christian friends I did a really good job of convincing them that I was 100 per cent committed to following God, but when I was at school with my friends I did a great job of convincing them that I was 100 per cent following the lifestyle that they followed. It was never an intentional decision to live like this: I just wanted to fit in. In my heart, I knew I wanted to follow God fully, but it felt so hard to do that among my non-Christian friends. 'Double agent' pretty much sums up how I was behaving.

I have to admit to a certain sense of trepidation as I'm writing this chapter. I am aware that this is a huge issue for many of the teenagers I know, but also for myself and my friends and other adults that I meet. The last thing I want to do is to pile heaps of guilt upon you, saying that you should be the next famous evangelist in your school and among your friends. Let us be clear: being a Christian at school or college, or in our sports teams or community groups, is rarely easy. People can have very set opinions about what Christians are like, mostly informed by characters in TV programmes, but sadly also by their experience of some Christians. Opening ourselves up to people's comments and opinions is a risky business, especially when what we really want is to be part of the group.

I have a memory firmly etched in my mind of going into a local secondary school to do an assembly (one of the joys of being a youth pastor!). The teacher introduced me and then asked all those in the hall who knew me to put their hands up and wave. I could sense people's hearts stopping and blood freezing in veins! Some quite happily did as was asked, but I could see others looking at me with pleading eyes, begging me to understand that they just couldn't do it. I really felt for the dilemma they were in: they didn't want to disown me but they didn't want their friends to ask how they knew me. What a nightmare!

For us, this opened up a lot of discussion about the double-agent business. I knew these teenagers; I knew their commitment to God and their love for him. I knew they were serious about their faith. At the same time, it was so hard to live out that faith at school and with their friends. Many of them confessed to feeling unhappy in both situations, church and school, because they knew they weren't being completely true to themselves (that 'integrity' word again).

It isn't God's desire that we should be the laughing stock among our peers. It is his desire, though, that all people should come to know him and to know his love for them. And he invites us to be part of his desire.

I used to think that being a missionary meant going abroad, probably to Africa, and telling people about Jesus. It came as quite a surprise to me to realize that God was asking me to be a missionary right where I was—in my school and in my home with my family. Going to Africa seemed a much easier option!

Have you considered that maybe God has put you in your school, college, hockey team, computer club or whatever for a reason? Look at the people around you: each one is somebody God loves, somebody he sent Jesus to die for and somebody he wants to reach. And the way that he plans to do that is through you.

An American writer, Dallas Willard, has a great definition of what it is to be a Christian. He explains it like this. As Christians, we are 'co-operative friends of Christ, living lives of constant, creative goodness'.[11] We are people who work alongside Jesus, loving and serving others so that they might see something of what he is like. That means doing it wherever we find ourselves. As Christian leaders, we in particular need to be taking this seriously. If we're to lead with integrity, then we need to be people who are consistently the same no matter where we are. It's a bit like being a stick of Blackpool rock: no matter where you cut it, you'll find the word 'Blackpool' running right through it.

My hope for my life is that wherever you meet me—whether in church, at work, going round the shops or out with friends—you will find the same person. I don't always manage it, but with God's help and the Holy Spirit changing me, that's what I'm working towards.

As we have already seen, if we are Christian leaders, we are leaders in all situations, not just when we play out our particular leadership role. So we're going to explore what that could look like, both in school or college and in our homes.

Leading at school or college

Pray

Probably the most important thing that you can do for your school or college is pray for it. Pray for the students there, for the teachers and for the support staff. Ask God to show you how he feels about these people, and look for ways in which you can serve and demonstrate God's care for them.

Prayer is amazing: not only does it change situations around us, but it also changes us. As we pray for different situations and people, very often our concern for them grows and we see them in a different light. Quite often, we can find that we're becoming the answer to our own prayers. Prayer also changes the way in which people look at us. I find that when I take time to pray about whatever I'm involved in and concerned about, I have a peace that I've not previously had. When I'm more peaceful and less anxious, that shows on my face and people can see the difference in my approach to things.

When my nephew started school, he wasn't always very happy about going. One day he was particularly upset, so my sister, his mum, suggested that they pray before he set off and ask Jesus to be there with him. His response was, 'That would be good, but I'd rather have someone that I could see.'

I know how he feels. Yet God's promise is that he is always with us and that we have the Holy Spirit within us, to give us confidence and courage and to remind us that God is right there too. Pray that you would know his presence and prompting as you go around your school or college.

I find it really helpful to write down specific issues or people that I'm praying for, so that I can be encouraged when I see God answer those prayers. Why not choose two or three people at school and start praying for them each day, and ask God for opportunities to serve them or even talk to them about him?

Connect with others

If there are others from your church, or from other churches, in your school, why not meet together every now and then, to pray and to encourage each other in the ways you see God at work? A group of students that I knew started doing this on a regular basis, and they found that many opportunities began opening up for them. As they prayed for their friends, their friends' attitudes started changing. They also found that it helped them with the double-agent life—or not living the double-agent life—because they had people who would ask them questions about how they were acting, and were also there to encourage them to keep going.

Influence others

Back in Chapter 1 we talked about the fact that one aspect of leadership means being people of influence. This is another key way in which we can be Christian leaders at school or college. We can have a positive influence on those around us. We can be those who look for people who are on the edge of things and invite them more into the centre, where stuff is happening. We can support events happening at school and encourage others who are taking part. I love it whenever any of our youth group are in a school performance, because we all go along to support them and cheer them on. We can demonstrate what it means to be good friends—friends who are trustworthy and speak well of others rather than putting them down.

I have a friend whom I have never heard say a bad word about anyone else. She constantly sees the best in people and loves to celebrate their achievements. She is a huge influence on me. When I'm around her, I'm far more conscious about the way I'm speaking of others than when I'm with those who are quite happy to point out the faults and failings of other people. You can be that kind of person, too, and it will have a huge influence on those around you.

There's a Bible passage that is helpful on this subject. 1 Peter 3:13–16 says:

Now, who will want to harm you if you are eager to do good? But even if you suffer for doing what is right, God will reward you for it. So don't worry or be afraid of their threats. Instead, you must worship Christ as Lord of your life. And if someone asks about your Christian hope, always be ready to explain it. But do this in a gentle and respectful way. Keep your conscience clear. Then if people speak against you, they will be ashamed when they see what a good life you live because you belong to Christ.

Peter is being honest about the difficulties that we sometimes face when living as Christians. At times we may suffer for our faith. At times people may ridicule us or speak against us. However, we need to make a choice about who we're living for: we can't be double agents.

In living the double-agent life we lose any sense of joy in our relationship with God as well as our relationship with our friends. We end up constantly feeling as if we're going to get found out. God is asking us to be bold enough to demonstrate that we're living a different life—not by becoming religious fanatics but by being people of hope, people of good influence and people who, day by day, are trying to live more as friends of Christ. I know this isn't easy but God promises that, as we take the risk, we will see him at work in our schools and colleges, and he will make up to us whatever we fear we might lose. However, we have to be willing to take that risk.

Tell the good news

A lot of what we've covered here has been about the way we live—our actions. But in the passage we read from 1 Peter 3, it also says that we need to be ready to respond to those who ask us about our 'Christian hope'—in other words, share our faith with them.

A friend of mine is about to head off to New York for a long weekend. Right now, if she mentions it one more time, I don't think I'm going to be responsible for my actions! She has managed to find a way of getting it into pretty much every conversation she's had for the last few weeks— with friends, the window cleaner, shop assistants. No matter what is being talked about, she finds a way of bringing it round to the news that she's going to New York. To her this is good news, and she wants to share it with anyone who will stand still long enough to listen.

Wouldn't it be great if that was how we felt about talking about God? The 'gospel' literally means 'good news'. It's good news because it talks of what God has done so that people can know him. It's good news because it changes lives radically. It's good news because it means we don't have to live another day of our lives without being in touch with the one who made us and who knows us best. So why do we find it so hard to share?

I guess part of it is fear of people's reactions to us, but I think it is also partly because we simply don't know how to share the gospel without tripping over ourselves or just sounding daft. A good place to start is by asking yourself these three questions:

❍ Why do you think it's good news?
❍ What difference has God made in your life?
❍ How does being a friend of God affect you day by day?

I think we sometimes need to rediscover for ourselves why it's such good news. Then it doesn't feel so much like something I 'ought to do' but instead is something that overflows from within us.

I was reflecting with a friend on why some of us find it quite easy to talk to others about God, and why for others it's a highly scary prospect. As a teenager, my friend was quite happy talking to his friends about Jesus, and so I tried to delve a bit deeper to find out why this was.

James wasn't brought up in a Christian family, but during his early teenage years he had an accident at school that left him unable to walk for a year. One Wednesday night, a Christian friend of the family came round and asked if he could pray for James. Although he didn't really understand what this meant, James said 'yes', and the guy simply prayed that God would heal his leg. Within the space of the evening, James was running up and down the stairs, his leg completely healed. Because of this experience of God at work, James and his parents became Christians.

People could actually see what God had done for James, and he was really happy to tell them. Some laughed at him for his faith, but that didn't sway him. Each day he could see the way in which God had worked, and, as the days and weeks and years went by, he could see how God continued to work—not always in as dramatic a way as when he first encountered God, but definitely at work all the same.

I think, for some of us, we love God and want to follow him, but it feels as if we have just head knowledge about God, rather than really knowing him. Those of you currently studying languages will know that in most languages other than English there are two verbs for 'to know'. One is to know something, like the French *savoir*, and the other is to know someone, like the French *connaître*.

We can learn a lot about God from the Bible and from those who teach us at church, and that is very important. But it's often only when we truly come to know (*connaître*) God—when we experience him in our everyday lives, not just read about stuff that he did long ago—that the good news of God starts to overflow from us. We're first-hand witnesses to what he's doing, and we've got a story to tell. So the good news becomes:

○ God has made us right with him because of Jesus' death on the cross.
○ Because Jesus was perfect, death couldn't keep hold of him and he rose to life and lives for ever.
○ God calls us his children and gives us his Holy Spirit.
○ The Holy Spirit helps us to become more like Jesus, and lets us know that God is constantly with us.
○ God longs to be part of our everyday lives, truly known by us, not just someone that we read about.

You might like to talk further with someone about this. If so, why not arrange to see your youth group leader, if you have one, or another adult that you know and trust? Also, do pray that God will help you to grow each day in your relationship with him. That is what he loves to do and, if you will let him, he will use you as you tell your story to your friends.

Leading at home

Being a Christian leader should also affect our home lives. In his book, *Help! I'm a Student Leader*, Doug Fields suggests that we can be people of 'upward influence'.[12] That means being people who influence those who are older than us, such as our parents or those who care for us in our homes.

Being a Christian leader at home has an interesting dynamic because this is the place where people get to see you exactly as you are, warts and all. These are the people who know your faults and failings as well as your strengths and achievements.

I was quite challenged recently about how my family always get the worst of me. I put on my best self when I'm with others. For example, I make sure that I'm awake enough to contribute fully to things outside the home, but when I go home to my family, I'm usually tired and really can't be bothered to make an effort at conversation or join in with what's happening. But my role as a Christian leader doesn't end when I walk through the door of my home. I need to be willing to serve there, too, and make family life a priority.

In our words

Something bizarre happens when you get into the teenage years. Your parents, who until this point may have been pretty much decent people, suddenly seem to come from another planet. Things that you once agreed on no longer seem so agreeable, and it can feel as if you're talking different languages on most subjects that you try to broach. In many ways this is quite natural: you're approaching adulthood and you are developing your own thoughts and opinions and becoming more independent, moving away from needing parental help quite so much. Sadly, for many teenagers, this becomes a time of major conflict.

As a young leader, you have a choice to make. You can simply decide that that's what the teenage years are about—settling for the belief that no one gets on with their parents or those responsible for them. Or you can decide to be someone who has 'upward influence'.

On a number of occasions, the Bible talks about obedience to parents as being an important part of honouring God (Romans 1:30; Ephesians 6:1; Colossians 3:20). It's not a hugely popular teaching, yet it's an important biblical principle. Obeying your parents is a key way of having upward influence. At the times when you don't agree with what they're saying, you have the choice of shouting and storming off, or staying put and talking matters through. And in those times when you can't come to a joint decision, maybe you could make the decision to go with their opinion. The more your parents see that you're willing to work with them, the more they will be able to trust you to make good decisions.

In our actions

Earlier we defined leadership as being an attitude of servanthood. That same attitude needs to extend to our family as well as those outside our homes. There are lots of simple ways in which we can demonstrate that we're leaders who are putting servanthood into action at home. First, this can be done by taking initiatives. Rather than waiting to be asked to do a certain job, why not surprise the people around you and just get on with it?

I know that at the end of the day all I want to do is collapse on the sofa and allow others to demonstrate their servant attitudes on my behalf. If I'm to have a positive influence, though, I need to be willing to get involved with the practical stuff at home and, if possible, before being asked to do so.

A great way to honour God and to show your leadership skills is to honour your family.

In our faith

When I first started as a youth pastor, we ran a Youth Alpha course for the 12- to 16-year-olds in the church, and also for those who had recently stopped coming to church. We had an excellent turnout and, over the following weeks, many of the young people either came to faith for the first time or came alive in their faith. This was great news for them as they discovered what it meant to have a relationship with God, and as they saw God at work in their friends. However, it was the knock-on effect in their families that was truly incredible to see.

Parents were noticing big changes and so were siblings, to the point where they were wanting to know more about God and faith for themselves. The youth group members were challenging their parents on the way they were living, and younger siblings were desperate to come and be part of the group.

When young people rise to the challenge of living as a Christian leader in all the situations where they find themselves, the response is often way beyond what you could ever imagine.

So, let's get back to Paul and Timothy. What advice does Paul give Timothy about living wholeheartedly as a Christian? In 2 Timothy 2, Paul uses three images to help Timothy understand.

○ **A soldier of Christ:** 'Soldiers don't get tied up in the affairs of civilian life, for then they cannot please the officer who enlisted them' (v. 4).
○ **A farmer:** 'Hardworking farmers should be the first to enjoy the fruit of their labour' (v. 6).
○ **An approved worker:** 'Be a good worker, one who does not need to be ashamed and who correctly explains the word of truth' (v. 15).

These are three very different images, but they all make the same point: we have to be focused on and committed to one thing only. As you read through particularly the second of Paul's letters to Timothy, you'll notice a recurring theme—suffering. He tells Timothy not to be ashamed of his (Paul's) suffering, and says that Timothy, too, should be ready to suffer for the gospel. This is hard to read, and I guess that Timothy wasn't over the moon about the prospect, but I love the fact that Paul was honest with Timothy about the cost of being a Christian and in particular being a Christian leader.

We may not have to suffer in the same way that Paul did (beatings and imprisonment) but I think I will have failed you if I don't mention something about the cost of being in Christian leadership. As you are probably already aware, it is sometimes really hard to be a Christian. Sometimes people misunderstand us or ridicule us for what we believe. Sometimes people go out of their way to make life difficult for us. But Paul's encouragement to us would be to stand strong, to endure it. Why? Because suffering is a good thing? I don't think so. I think it's because Paul knows that it is worth it in the end.

Living the double-agent life is exhausting and highly unsatisfying, whereas Jesus' promise is that those who follow him will have 'life to the full', 'life in all abundance' (John 10:10). This doesn't mean that life will always be easy, but it does mean that if we trust him, and if we take risks in being open about who we are and who we're following, we will know a joy that just can't be compared with anything else. We may lose a couple of friends along the way but what we will gain is so much greater.

Wrapping it up

In God's kingdom, being a double agent is not an option. It's not that God is desperately trying to make life hard for us. He knows that when we try to serve two masters, we end up failing them both. He intends us to know real joy in following him, and the privilege of being part of his work among the people around us.

Ready to lead

To think about:

○ How do you relate to the picture of the double agent?
○ Have you recently been in a situation where it was hard for you to stand up as a Christian? What did you do?

To do:

○ Surprise your family this week by doing something unexpected (in a good way!)

○ Arrange to meet with one or two of your friends to pray for your school or college.

The bigger picture

Hi Ruth

You're not going to believe this, but I've just been to the most amazing church service! This week, instead of going out to CYFA, we stayed in church because we had a visiting speaker.

To be honest with you, I thought I was going to be completely bored out of my brains. The speaker was an elderly woman who has just returned to England after spending 40 years in India. The stories she told were incredible—she's spent pretty much all of her life working with people who have absolutely nothing, helping them get to know God but also making sure they have the physical things that they need.

It was so inspiring and really opened my eyes. I've never really thought much about what I could do to help in those situations, but now I can't stop thinking about it. It all feels a bit overwhelming. Have you ever thought about this stuff?

Mmmmmm, how to respond?

What do you think? Would you suggest...

○ that they forget about it all, because the inspiration will soon pass?
○ that they find a project locally that they could get involved with?

○ that they immediately sell everything they own and send the money to India?
○ that they gather some friends together to investigate how they could be involved with an overseas project?
○ that they ask God to keep them open to the needs of others throughout the rest of their life?
○ something else?

*

At the time of writing his second letter to Timothy, Paul was being held as a prisoner of the state because he'd been travelling around preaching the gospel, the good news of Jesus. Despite the knowledge that he is soon to be condemned to death, he still encourages Timothy to do the leadership work that God has given him to do. He exhorts Timothy not to be ashamed of his work, and not to be ashamed about Paul being in prison: 'So never be ashamed to tell others about our Lord. And don't be ashamed of me, either, even though I'm in prison for him. With the strength God gives you, be ready to suffer with me for the sake of the Good News' (2 Timothy 1:8).

Being imprisoned for talking about Jesus wasn't common only in the Roman empire at the time of the early Church. The situation continues today. For hundreds of thousands of Christians around the world, persecution for their faith is part of daily experience. Many are imprisoned or even killed simply because of what they believe. For many of them, the mere fact of owning a Bible would put them in prison. Countless people are rejected by their friends and families because they've converted to Christianity, and have to live each day with the awareness that meeting other Christians puts them in real danger.

In May 2005, news broke across the world of three Indonesian women who had been arrested, tried and sentenced to three years' imprisonment. Their crime was running a 'Happy Sunday' club, a Sunday school programme that a local primary school had asked them to run for its Christian students. The problems arose when it was discovered that they had allowed Muslim children to come to the club. Even though the children had their parents' consent to be there, the Muslim leaders in the town filed a complaint with the police, and the women were found guilty of 'Christianization'. On 1 September 2005 they began their three-year sentence.

One of the women was concerned about what the news would do to her elderly father. However, this was his response:

I'm proud of my daughter, proud of the suffering she has to go through for Christ. So be firm, keep doing God's will, keep spreading the gospel of the love of Christ, without fear. And now I will go about the village and tell everyone that my child is in prison and that I am proud of her.

As we read what Paul has to say to Timothy, we can hear him asking Timothy to have the same response: 'Don't be ashamed of me, keep on with sharing the good news of Jesus, and don't ever be ashamed of it.' The writer to the Hebrews also picks up this theme. In Hebrews 13.3 he says, 'Don't forget about those in prison. Suffer with them as though you were there yourself. Share the sorrow of those being mistreated.'

We are so fortunate in the UK. We still have complete freedom to meet together as Christians, to have Bibles in our homes and to be able to share our faith with others. It is true that it is getting harder to be a Christian here, but compared with other countries we have immense opportunities. Those of us who don't suffer persecution because of following Jesus are actually in the minority.

With this freedom that we have comes responsibility. Paul would encourage us to remember those who are in prison for their faith, those who are being persecuted. This is an area where, as Christian leaders, we must take the lead. We have the responsibility to keep ourselves and others informed of what's happening to those who share our faith—those whom the Bible would call our 'brothers and sisters' around the world—and to demonstrate a real care and concern for them.

There are a number of ways in which we can do this. If you type "persecuted church" into Google, you will find lots of resources to inform you about the situations in different countries, and many organizations to inform you about how you can encourage and act on behalf of those suffering persecution. A number of the organizations have websites aimed at teenagers, which offer very useful resources to help you be informed and active on behalf of the persecuted church (for example, see http://underground.opendoorsuk.org).

Passionate about justice

In 2 Timothy 1:8, Paul is talking particularly about suffering for sharing the gospel, but, as God's people and especially as leaders, we need to care about persecution and injustice in their many forms. God cares passionately about justice and wants his people to share that concern. An American Christian activist and speaker, Jim Wallis, tells how a fellow student at his Bible college took hold of an old Bible and cut out every single reference to justice and poverty. Wallis says that when the student was done, that Bible was literally in shreds, falling apart in his hands. It was a Bible full of holes.

God has much to say on the subject of injustice and the poor. Bible Society has just produced a Bible that, rather than cutting out all the passages referring to justice and poverty, has highlighted them. You can barely turn a page without finding a highlighted passage. Here are a few of them to give you a feel for what God says:

If you really want to live, you must stop doing wrong and start doing right. I, the Lord God All-Powerful, will then be on your side, just as you claim I am. Choose good instead of evil! See that justice is done.
AMOS 5:14–15 (CEV)

But you must defend those who are helpless and have no hope. Be fair and give justice to the poor and homeless.
PROVERBS 31:8–9 (CEV)

The Lord your God is more powerful than all other gods and lords, and his tremendous power is to be feared. His decisions are always fair, and you cannot bribe him to change his mind. The Lord defends the rights of orphans and widows. He cares for foreigners and gives them food and clothing. And you should also care for them, because you were foreigners in Egypt.
DEUTERONOMY 10:17–19 (CEV)

Sometimes God has difficult words for his people to hear:

I, the Lord, hate and despise your religious celebrations and your times of worship. I won't accept your offerings or animal sacrifices—not even your very best. No more of your noisy songs! I won't listen when you play your harps. But let justice and fairness flow like a river that never runs dry.
AMOS 5:21–24 (CEV)

Here God is saying that if you really are worshipping him, then you will care about justice. It's not that he doesn't want our worship; it's just that If it isn't backed up with a concern for what he cares about, the worship is no more than empty words, and he's definitely not into that.

In Micah 6:8, one of the best-known verses on this subject, the prophet outlines what it means to be a follower of God. 'The Lord God has told us what is right and what he demands: "See that justice is done, let mercy be your first concern, and humbly obey your God"' (CEV). I find this verse very helpful when thinking about what God is asking me to do. In the times when I'm not quite sure where he's leading, I know that wherever I am, this verse describes what he asks of me and what is pleasing to him.

How can we put this into action? I often feel overwhelmed when I consider the amount of injustice and poverty in the world. I wonder what on earth I can do, as one ordinary person. But throughout history, God has used ordinary individuals, people like you and me, to speak out against injustice and take action for those in need. Rather than letting ourselves be overwhelmed, we can ask ourselves what the issues are that need confronting in the world today.

○ People-trafficking?
○ Unfair working conditions for children in the Two-Thirds World?
○ Famine?
○ Lack of basic human resources?
○ Children being forced into life as soldiers?

Why not ask God to show you what you could do in one of these situations? There is a lot that we feel we can't change, but there is so much that we can do. God's intention is that his people will carry the same concern that he has for those in need, and you can lead the way in this.

Your kingdom come

I guess that the Lord's Prayer is pretty familiar to most of us. The problem with something familiar, though, is that we can stop hearing the words. Within the Lord's Prayer there are some amazing statements that we pray on a regular basis. Try reading through the Lord's Prayer slowly and reflecting on each statement:

Our Father in Heaven,
Hallowed be your name.
Your kingdom come, your will be done
On earth as it is in heaven.
Give us this day our daily bread
And forgive us our sins,
as we forgive those who sin against us.
Lead us not into temptation
But deliver us from evil.
For the kingdom, the power and the glory are yours
Now and for ever. Amen.

Jesus gave this prayer as an outline to his disciples when they asked him how to pray, and there are some big themes captured within it. The lines that I would like to focus on for a moment are 'Your kingdom come, your will be done on earth as it is in heaven.' This is a phrase that I've been thinking about a lot lately. When you unpack it, what we are requesting is quite spectacular. Basically, it's saying, 'Please let heaven come to earth. Let all the good things to do with heaven be present here on earth, now, today.' In the three years of Jesus' earthly ministry, he spent a lot of his time going around telling people that 'the kingdom of God is near', and he demonstrated it by healing the lame, curing the sick, delivering people from demons and raising the dead. He was making heaven happen on earth, and he invites us to share in that work today.

In Matthew 5—7, a passage known as the Sermon on the Mount, Jesus talks a lot about what his kingdom should look like. He talks about the way we should act towards others, the way we should deal with those who stand against us and, primarily, how his followers can live generous lives.

'Let me tell you why you are here. You're here to be salt-seasoning that brings out the God-flavours of this earth. If you lose your saltiness, how will people taste godliness? ... Here's another way to put it: You're here to be light, bringing out the God-colours in the world. God is not a secret to be kept. We're going public with this, as public as a city on a hill. If I make you light-bearers, you don't think I'm going to hide you under a bucket, do you? I'm putting you on a light stand. Now that I've put you there on a hilltop, on a light stand—shine! Keep open house; be generous with your lives. By opening up to others, you'll prompt people to open up with God, this generous Father in heaven.' (5:13–16, THE MESSAGE)

Along with a group of friends, I've started looking at different situations and asking, 'What would this place look like if the kingdom of God was here?' Because, you see, being a Christian isn't only about telling others the good news of Jesus; it's about being good news.

Some friends have recently returned from a trip to Chennai in South India, where they were visiting some of the Dalit people. The Dalit people are considered to be the lowest of the low in the caste system and were traditionally known as the 'untouchables'. As a result, they are ostracized socially, they live in poverty and they have no voice politically. In Chennai there is what's known as 'the river' running through the town, but really it is just an open sewer, and the Dalit people are living along its banks.

On returning from their trip to Chennai, my friends started asking the question, 'What would it look like for the kingdom of God to come to Chennai?' Part of their response was that the sewer would be cleaned up and made into a proper river, full of fresh water and a good place to live beside. They're now exploring ways in which this can be made a reality. That's just one example of God's people taking seriously Jesus' commission to them to proclaim that the kingdom of God is near, and that as things are in heaven, so they should be on earth.

Local and global

This should be the concern of all God's people but, as leaders, we have an extra responsibility of using the leadership gifts that God has given us to act on behalf of others, and to inspire others to do the same. You are the ones with influence, the ones who will inspire others to follow your example and get on board with different issues and causes. As leaders, we are not just to be people who talk about God, but people who believe that God wants to change things and will use us to do so.

Can I encourage you to engage with issues around the world, to engage with the people of the persecuted church and to get active in responding to some of the many needs out there? Could you link your youth group or friends at school to an organization that is working to relieve the poverty and suffering of people around the world? Can you get yourself informed about some of these situations and take time to pray? Can you write letters, and encourage others to do the same, to heads of governments who have the power to bring about nationwide change?

Just after Jesus rose to life, and before he was taken into heaven, he commissioned his disciples to go out into all the world to tell others about him and the kingdom of God. He told them to go to Jerusalem, throughout Judea, to Samaria and to the ends of the earth (Acts 1:8). This is a really good model for us to use: Jerusalem was where they were, Judea was the surrounding area, Samaria was the place beyond that, and the 'ends of the earth' were even further beyond. As we think about being leaders in the bigger picture, we should be asking ourselves what the needs are in the places where we live, in the communities that we're part of and, beyond those, in the rest of the UK, Europe and the world.

Wrapping it up

Leadership is not just about leading in our particular role. It's about having a bigger vision of what God longs to do in the world, and how we can play our part and enable others to play theirs too. Christian leadership is about dreaming big dreams, dreams so big that to our human minds they seem impossible, yet with God's intervention they can become a reality. Christian leadership is about gathering a group of people around you who will dream big dreams with you and work together with God to make them happen.

Ready to lead

To think about:

○ What causes do you feel strongly about?
○ What would it look like for the 'kingdom to come' in an area of your community?

To do:

○ Research an organization that works with the persecuted church and find out how you can get involved.
○ Prepare some information on a particular cause or situation to present to your youth group or give to your friends.

8

Sharing the journey

Dear Ruth

I don't know if you remember me—we met at the young leaders' conference at Easter. I found it a really useful time but I still have a number of questions about some things that I'm involved in here.

Actually, I have lots of questions, but I'm not sure who to ask about them. My parents try to give me advice, but I don't think they really get where I'm coming from.

Do you have any ideas about who I could go to, or how I can find someone that would be willing to help me with my questions?

Look forward to hearing from you.

Mmmmmm, how to respond?

What do you think? Would you suggest...

○ that they learn to find the answers to their questions themselves?
○ that they come straight round to see you and you'll sort them out?
○ that they offload all their worries and concerns to the guy at church who's just become a Christian?
○ that they ask their church minister if there's someone he or she could recommend?
○ that they just stop stressing and get on with stuff?
○ something else?

*

You have heard me teach things that have been confirmed by many reliable witnesses. Now teach these truths to other trustworthy people who will be able to pass them on to others.

2 TIMOTHY 2:2

You, Timothy, certainly know what I teach, and how I live, and what my purpose in life is. You know my faith, my patience, my love, and my endurance... You must remain faithful to the things you have been taught. You know they are true, for you know you can trust those who taught you.

2 TIMOTHY 3:10, 14

The other week, I was leading a seminar for a group of churches. Among the group was someone I've known for quite a long time, and at the end of the session he greeted me with the words 'I can so see who's mentored you!' Now, he had no definite knowledge of who that person was. He could just see, in the way I did things, in the way I spoke and probably even in my hand gestures, something of the person who has influenced me and taught me so much about what I now do—and he was spot on!

The person he was talking about has been my mentor for quite a long time now, and has had a huge impact on my life. I still meet with her on a regular basis and she continues to inspire, challenge and teach me.

There is currently a lot of talk about mentoring, with many schools setting up mentoring programmes for their students, but it's actually not a new thing. Mentoring has been around pretty much since the beginning of time, and it is something that God has used through the generations to build up leaders and disciples. It could also be considered as part of the approach that Jesus used in order to develop his disciples. It's fascinating, as you read the Gospel writers' accounts of Jesus' ministry (in Matthew, Mark, Luke and John), to see how much time Jesus spent with just a few people. As you read the stories, you will find that in the midst of travelling around, teaching the crowds and healing the sick, Jesus spent a phenomenal amount of time with the twelve disciples, and out of those twelve he chose three in whom to invest the most time—Peter, James and John.

Throughout the Bible you can trace a chain of mentoring relationships:

○ Jethro (Moses' father-in-law) mentored Moses.
○ Moses mentored Joshua and the elders of Israel.
○ Joshua mentored other army leaders.
○ Deborah mentored the army commander, Barak.
○ Eli mentored Samuel.
○ Samuel mentored Saul and David, who became the greatest king Israel had ever known.
○ David mentored Solomon.
○ Solomon mentored the queen of Sheba, who took his wisdom back to her people in the form of the Proverbs.
○ Elijah mentored Elisha.
○ Elisha mentored King Jehoash.
○ Daniel mentored King Nebuchadnezzar.
○ Mordecai mentored his niece Esther, resulting in the deliverance of God's people.
○ Jesus mentored the twelve disciples who established the Christian Church.
○ Barnabas mentored Paul.
○ Paul mentored Timothy and Titus, among others, resulting in dozens of new churches in Asia.

What do we mean by 'mentoring'?

Mentoring takes different forms depending on the context but, within the context of Christian leadership that we're considering, it could be defined as a relationship in which one person helps another to grow in their faith and leadership ability by sharing the God-given resources of skills, wisdom, knowledge and experience.

Mentoring is an intentional relationship—that is to say, it won't just happen by accident. The people involved are clear about why they're meeting and, although there is a large element of friendship involved, it's a relationship with a specific purpose.

Mentoring is also a relationship where permission is given to the mentor to ask difficult questions of the person being mentored, about their relationship with family, friends and God. If there's not a willingness to be open and honest about the way things are, the mentoring relationship becomes ineffective.

However, it's worth saying that mentoring is not about being told what to do. It's about learning together and being given space and time to reflect with someone else listening in, who offers help and guidance along the way.

Why is mentoring important?

There is so much that we can learn about leadership by reading books on the subject or listening to talks, but a lot of leadership is 'caught' by us rather than 'taught' to us. As we spend time with other leaders, we learn a lot from them about how they respond in different situations and how they stay close to God, and we can learn from them practical skills of leadership.

This seems to be how Jesus did it with the disciples. They spent time together and would have seen Jesus respond to the religious rulers who set out to trip him up; they would have seen him dealing compassionately with those who came to him for healing, and from him they learnt how to serve others.

This also seems to be the model that Paul used in Thessalonica. When he writes to the Christians there, he's able to reflect on his time with them and say this:

We were like a mother feeding and caring for her own children. We loved you so much that we shared with you not only God's Good News but our own lives too. Don't you remember, dear brothers and sisters, how hard we worked among you? ... You yourselves are our witnesses—and so is God—that we were devout and honest and faultless towards all of you believers. And you know that we treated each of you as a father treats his own children. We pleaded with you, encouraged you, and urged you to live your lives in a way that God would consider worthy. For he called you to share in his Kingdom and glory. (1 Thessalonians 2:7–12, abridged)

Mentoring is important because it's a key way not only of sharing information, but of sharing our lives, and being able to see in action what it means to be a Christian leader. This is the relationship that Paul had with Timothy. They would have travelled around a lot together and Timothy would have seen Paul in action, and he would also have taken part in setting up new churches. Paul wanted Timothy to remember all that he'd learnt and not keep it for himself but to pass it on to others who were also involved in leadership.

In a church that I was part of at one time, I asked the members of the youth group whether there was any particular area of the church's life where they would like to be involved. The responses were many and varied. Some people wanted to be involved in the music group, some wanted to learn how to use the sound system, and others wanted to be part of the prayer ministry team. We partnered each one with someone who was already in the team that they wanted to join, so that they could learn from them. The young people involved felt that they grew far more through these relationships than by simply trying on their own.

For us as leaders, it's important to learn from other leaders how to grow the leadership skills that we have, and also how to grow as disciples. Intentionally spending time with people in leadership roles will give us an insight into how they work things out in their daily lives, how they make good decisions, and how they use their gifts and skills to serve others.

Mentoring is also important because it keeps us focused on where God is leading us. If we've started leading at a young age, it means that we should have many years ahead of us in which to grow in leadership. If we're going to grow well, stay committed to God and keep fresh in our leadership, we need others alongside us to encourage and cheer us, inspiring us to keep aiming to be all that God created us to be.

This is Connie's story.

When I was 14, I became a Christian after always having gone to church without realizing that Jesus wanted to know me or that I could know him too. I was a very insecure girl without any idea of self-worth, who looked for identity in anything or anyone. My parents had split up when I was 11 and it had turned my world upside down. When I first felt God, all I could do was cry, and it continued like that for a long time. My youth pastor, who became my mentor, got alongside me and met up with me every week during my teenage years. She taught me so much about God and encouraged me to keep looking to him. I feel that God brought her into my life to show me love and to cause me to trust when I felt betrayed. With her support I have been able to overcome many challenges and become more of the person God created me to be. I've discovered more about the gifts that God has given me, that he has asked me to be a leader, and we're exploring how I can use those gifts.

Different mentoring relationships

What's great about mentoring relationships is that they can happen in a number of different contexts. The pattern set out in the Bible seems to be that as you reach out to someone ahead of you to teach, encourage and inspire you, you should also be stretching out a hand to someone younger than you, whom you can mentor. Each one of us has plenty to learn from someone else and plenty to offer to someone coming up behind us. One of the things I enjoy most is mentoring three younger women who are youth pastors. At first I wondered if I had anything to offer them, but God uses the different experiences that we have and the skills that he's growing in us to encourage others.

We can also be mentored by people that we'll never meet. We can do this by reading biographies of other Christian leaders and learning from their lives. In recent weeks, I've read three, all of which have inspired me in different ways. The first was an autobiography of a Christian businesswoman, Carly Fiorina.[13] She tells her story of working within the business world and how she developed leadership skills there. The second book was the biography of Amy Carmichael, a missionary to India.[14] Amy died a long time ago but the story of her life and her commitment to following God into some really dark places has challenged me enormously. The third book was the one I mentioned earlier, by Kay Warren, about the way she was awakened to the AIDS pandemic. Again, it was hugely challenging and inspiring.[15] As I have spent time with these three women, through reading about them rather than meeting them, I have learnt so much from them. I feel encouraged to grow in my relationship with God, and to use my skills and gifts to serve others.

We can also mentor each other as friends. I meet with a couple of friends on a regular basis, when we have a meal together, take a look at a Bible passage, reflect on how the last couple of weeks have been and then pray for each other and for our church.

So at the moment my mentoring network looks something like this:

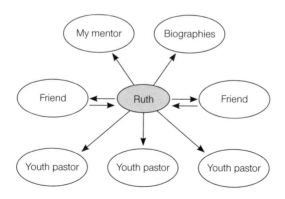

What does mentoring involve?

Mentoring can involve a number of different elements, depending on what you want to get out of it. These elements can include:

- ○ reading the Bible together.
- ○ reflecting on life since the last time you met—how your relationships have been, where you have known God prompting you, anything that hasn't been so good, and so on.
- ○ reflecting on leadership opportunities that you (or they—if you're mentoring others) have had, lessons learnt and so on.
- ○ deciding on a book that you will both read and then discussing it together.
- ○ praying together.
- ○ setting goals for the coming weeks and months.
- ○ offering encouragement.
- ○ discussing particular issues that you're facing.
- ○ eating together.
- ○ doing some activity or leadership task together.
- ○ listening.
- ○ celebrating good stuff that has happened.

What to look for in a mentor

It's really important that your mentor is someone you trust and respect, someone you feel you will be able to talk with easily and openly. They need to be good at listening, and not desperate always to give you advice and tell you what to do. The role of a good mentor is to enable you to think things through and listen to where God might be leading you. It's always a good plan to meet a couple of times to see how you get on, before making a long-term commitment, so that either one can pull out if they feel the chemistry isn't there. On a practical level, your mentor also needs to be someone who has the time to take on this responsibility.

I meet my mentor once a month for an hour and a half, which seems to work really well for us. One of the first conversations that is useful to have is about where and when you will meet. And don't forget to make sure your parents know where you are and who you're with!

Your mentor should be someone who is following Jesus themselves and committed to growing as a Christian disciple. It's also useful if they have experience in the same kind of leadership as you. So if you're involved in the children's ministry at church, it would be good to have an older and more experienced children's worker as your mentor. If your main leadership role happens out on the sports field, see if you can find someone else who is involved in that area.

If there really doesn't seem to be anyone who shares your leadership interest, do still look out for a mentor, because even if they don't share exactly the same experience there will still be much to be gained. Have a look around in your church to see if there is anyone you think would be suitable, inform your parents and ask them to come with you to ask that person if they would be your mentor. If you're unable to spot anyone, why not ask your parents, your youth leader or your church leader if there is anyone that they could suggest?

On being a mentor

In order to be a mentor, we have to reflect the same sort of characteristics as listed above in terms of what we should look for in a mentor. We should be committed to our own spiritual growth, and we should want to serve others, not merely tell them what to do. We should be trustworthy and able to respect the confidence of those we're mentoring.

One of the key skills of an effective mentor is the ability to ask good questions. I try to listen closely to the questions that my mentor asks me, or the questions I hear other people asking, and make a note of them. I then use them with the people I'm mentoring. I also pray before I meet up with them and ask God to give me wisdom about what sort of questions to ask.

Wrapping it up

One of the great privileges that we have as God's people is sharing each other's lives. Right from the start, God's intention was that we should have companionship, to experience the good things that come from being with others. Mentoring is an excellent way of tapping into some of the amazing wisdom that people have, and of being able to share with others the wisdom and experience that God is growing in you.

Signing off

It feels like we've travelled a long way since the start of this book. If you've made it to the end, congratulations! Let's finish with a final word from Paul. As he comes to the end of his second letter to Timothy, he knows that the end of his life is in view and he takes a moment to reflect on all that he's done:

As for me, my life has already been poured out as an offering to God. The time of my death is near. I have fought a good fight, I have finished the race, and I have remained faithful. And now the prize awaits me—the crown of righteousness, which the Lord, the righteous Judge, will give me on the day of his return. And the prize is not just for me but for all who eagerly look forward to his glorious return. (2 Timothy 4:6–8)

In writing these letters to Timothy, Paul was trying to encapsulate good leadership advice for him, and also to encourage Timothy to stay faithful to his calling from God. Paul longed for Timothy to live out his entire life following God, so that at the end he would be able to reflect on the years that had passed and say the same as Paul. Paul was very clear about his focus—receiving the crown that God promises to all who faithfully follow him—and he wanted Timothy to have that focus too.

I am so thankful for the people who have crossed my path over the years, who have encouraged me and inspired me to keep my eyes fixed on Jesus, who have helped me to discover the gifts and skills that God has placed in me and have given me opportunities to use those gifts to serve the church. Those people have been to me as Paul was to Timothy. I know, too, that if I'm to stay faithful through the years to come, I will continue to need people like that in my life.

My prayer for you, as our paths have crossed through the pages of this book, is that you would hear me cheering you on, encouraging you to discover the person that God has created you to be. I pray that you would celebrate the gifts and skills he has put within you and that you will be surrounded by others who can give you the opportunity to grow in your gifts. Keep your eyes fixed on Jesus, keep company with those who will inspire you to stay close to him, and keep on serving those who know him and also those who don't, praying that through your life something of his power and glory would be seen. And above all, revel in the fact that God calls you his own.

Ready to lead

To think about:

○ As you look at the life of your church, is there something you'd like to be involved with? Who could you talk to about this?

○ What does your mentoring network look like at the moment? What could you do to grow it?

To do:

○ Read a biography of a Christian leader.

○ Identify a younger person that you could mentor and see how they feel about the idea.

✻

Appendix

Descriptions of spiritual gifts

Gift	Description	Bible reference	You?
Administration	To organize	1 Corinthians 12:28	
Apostle	To perceive the big picture and pioneer new things	Ephesians 4:11	
Discerning spirits	To discern whether or not something is from God	1 Corinthians 12:10	
Evangelist	To communicate the good news effectively to people who are not Christians	Ephesians 4:11	
Exhortation	To encourage others	Romans 12:8	
Faith	To trust confidently in God for particular things	1 Corinthians 12:9	
Giving	To provide resources for people's needs	Romans 12:8	
Healing	To call on God to heal supernaturally	1 Corinthians 12:9, 28	
Helps	To help others	1 Corinthians 12:28 Romans 12:7	
Interpretation of tongues	To understand and communicate the meaning of an unknown language	1 Corinthians 12:10	
Knowledge	To know God's way forward	1 Corinthians 12:8	
Leadership	To set a vision for others and motivate others to fulfil it	Romans 12:8	
Mercy	To empathize with people who are hurt, and provide practical help so as to encourage those in need	Romans 12:8	
Miracles	To call on God to do supernatural acts	1 Corinthians 12:10, 28	
Pastor	To care for the growth of believers	Ephesians 4:11	
Prophecy	To speak out truth from God in order to encourage or correct believers and to encourage non-Christians to accept God's truth	1 Corinthians 12:10 Romans 12:6	
Teaching	To understand and communicate the truth of God in a clear and relevant way	Romans 12:7	
Tongues	To speak an unknown language	1 Corinthians 12:10	
Wisdom	To discern God's way forward in complex situations	1 Corinthians 12:8	

ADAPTED FROM THE GROWING LEADERS COURSE (CPAS, 2006)

Notes

1   Definition of talent taken from James Lawrence, *Growing Leaders* (BRF, 2004), p. 25.

2   Dorothy C. Bass and Don C. Richter, *Way to Live* (Upper Room Books, 2002), p. 16.

3   Words spoken by Thomas Merton on the night before his final trip to Asia.

4   C.S. Lewis, *Mere Christianity* (Fount, 1983).

5   Bass and Richter, *Way to Live*, p. 287.

6   Bill Hybels, *Who You Are When No One's Looking* (Kingsway, 1987), p. 7.

7   Ibid., p. 21.

8   Rien Poortvliet, *The Ark* (Lion, 1985).

9   Rick Warren, *The Purpose-Driven Church* (Zondervan, 1996).

10 Doug Fields, *Help! I'm a Student Leader* (Zondervan, 2005), p. 66.

11 Dallas Willard, *The Divine Conspiracy* (Fount, 1998), p. 30.

12 Fields, *Help! I'm a Student Leader*, p. 104.

13 Carly Fiorina, *Tough Choices* (Nicholas Brealey Publishing, 2006)

14 Frank L. Houghton, *Amy Carmichael of Dohnavur* (Hodder, 1988).

15 Kay Warren, *Dangerous Surrender* (Zondervan, 2007).

CPAS is an Anglican evangelical mission agency working with churches, mainly in the UK and Republic of Ireland.

CPAS enables churches to help every person hear and discover the good news of Jesus.

CPAS
Athena Drive
Tachbrook Park
WARWICK
CV34 6NG
01926 458458
info@cpas.org.uk
www.cpas.org.uk

The Arrow Leadership Programme aims to develop Christian leaders for the Church of the 21st century. It is not merely another course or conference—its aim is 'life transformation'. Over 18 months, Arrow helps participants to grow through teaching, reflection, worship, interaction, application, accountability and fun.

For further information visit www.cpas.org.uk/arrow or call CPAS.

brf

Resourcing your spiritual journey

through...

- Bible reading notes
- Books for Advent & Lent
- Books for Bible study and prayer
- Books to resource those working with under 11s in school, church and at home

- Quiet days and retreats
- Training for primary teachers and children's leaders
- Godly Play
- Barnabas RE Days

For more information, visit the **brf** website at **www.brf.org.uk**

BRF is a Registered Charity